Zulu Boy Gone Crazy

Hilarious tales post Polokwane

FRED KHUMALO

KMM REVIEW PUBLISHING

Johannesburg

Published in 2010 by
KMM REVIEW PUBLISHING COMPANY (PTY) Ltd
PO Box 78214, Sandton, 2146

ISBN 987-0-620-44889-5

Book design and layout: Culture Publishing Industry
Cover design: Culture Publishing Industry
Editing: Pat Tucker

Printing and Binding: Colors

Some of these columns were first published in the Sunday Times.
The author and publisher would like to thank Mr. Mondli Makhanya
and Avusa Media for their support of this project.

CONTENTS

PREFACE

In October 1827 the flesh and spirit of Queen Nandi, mother to the great Zulu emperor Shaka, parted ways. A period of mourning was subsequently declared by the then Zulu state prime minister, Ngomane. During this period – a year in total – no cultivation of crops, consumption of meat or drinking of milk was permitted. Three months into this strictly-enforced ordinance, the nation was in the grip of a protracted, debilitating mourning season ordered by the inconsolable Shaka. This nation he had ruthlessly and meticulously constructed was hurtling towards certain demise.

While those in the inner royal circles dilly-dallied and obfuscated, it took the courage of an outsider, a certain Gala kaNodade of the Biyelas, to whisper this reality into the great Shaka's ear before he was faced with the threat of the impending destruction of his kingdom. But more than anything else, it was Gala's eloquence that won the day. Gala kaNodade employed flowery language and Zulu idiomatic prose to hypnotise the great Shaka – a ruse called ukuluma uphephetha (biting hard while blowing gently on the wound).

This is the role that the columnist is meant to play; coaxing, leading us and gently cajoling us towards the hard truths of our existence. This is the domain that Fred Khumalo has made his own through his column in the Fred Khumalo Page of the Sunday Times. Khumalo is the archetypical rabble-rouser. He revels in his self-appointed role of setting the cat among the pigeons, if only to elicit a response from the cat and the pigeons that either validates or dismisses the veracity of their feline or avian natures respectively.

With tongue firmly in cheek, mischievous glint in his eye and impish countenance, Fred meticulously sets about challenging us to interrogate our true nature as a species. That is, after all, the core function of the columnist - to dissect societal existential truths and drag the citizens kicking and screaming closer to facing their demons. Fred's columns are laced with a self-effacing, disarming glibness that successfully masks the underlying steeliness of his probing, razor-edged writing feather.

But more than anything else, true to the 'Somewhat serious, somewhat fun' tag, Fred Khumalo has the enviable gift of being entertaining as he goes about disseminating these truths. The effortless eloquence of his prose reveals the existence of a bonafide, first tier novelist bubbling just underneath the surface which often leaves one with a sense of guilt, as if enjoying a first class flight using an economy class ticket.

When I grow up, I want to write like Fred Khumalo.

Ndumiso Ngcobo, author of Some of My Best Friends Are White and Is it 'Coz I'm Black?

Zulu Dawn

Zulu Dawn

NOW THAT WE HAVE A 100% ZULU PERSON as president, who dances, sings, laughs, tells stories at the slightest provocation, I can safely assume that it's cool to be Zulu. In response to floods of enquiries from South Africans of non-Zulu extraction who are dying to understand the Zulu psyche, I have put together a short A to Z idiot's guide to the state of being Zulu.

So, here goes:

A is for *Amabele* — in our language amabele means two things: sorghum, which is beloved by us as we can make porridge out of it, but we can also make sorghum beer. Sorghum beer makes us jovial. The other meaning of amabele is: women's breasts, which, as any proud Zulu man can confirm, are also beloved by us.

B is for *Bhaxabula* — to beat a person vehemently, a favourite Zulu pastime. The synonyms for (uku)bhaxabula are (uku)bhibiza, or (uku)bhonya.

C is for (UKU)*Cula* – singing. Singing, as the new president has demonstrated, is very close to our hearts. But C is also for Clegg, Johnny Clegg. This visionary white man saw the light a long time ago — and became a genuine Zulu man at a time when it was not fashionable to wear Zulu garb in public places.

D is for (ISI)*Dudula* — a firm woman with a nice, well-formed behind and good amabele – a true African woman.

E is for *Ehhe* — which means 'yes'. We like saying 'ehhe', especially when the full sentence is: 'ehhe, ngiyaphinda ngithi ngizokushaya (yes, I am saying it again, I am going to donner you!').

F is for *Fihliza* — to demolish. Just what the ANC did to the opposition in the last election.

G is for (UKU)*Gida* — traditional dancing, as ably demonstrated by our new president.

H is for (E)*Hositela* – that's where many of our men choose to reside, the hostels. **H is also (I)*Hlongandlebe*** — one who is so stubborn it seems as if he was dropped on his head when he was young. In other words, Julius Malema, president of the African National Congress Youth League.

I is for *Inyoka* — snake. We hate snakes with a passion — especially if the snake in question is actually a person; an untrustworthy person, especially when he holds a differing political viewpoint. I is also for imbongi – a poet. Zulus love a good poet — especially the opposite of Mzwakhe Mbuli, Mbuli, Mbuli (the 'people's poet' who likes repeating things thrice).

J is for (I)Jele — that's jail to you. We are afraid of jail, but our predilection for ukubhaxabula (see above) always lands us in (e)jele.

K is for Khumalo — the loveliest people on earth, as long as you don't mess with them.

L is for (I)Landi — that is rand to you, the stuff that you produce when you are buying something at the shop. We have great respect for (i)landi and we go to great lengths to acquire it. Some say we steal ilandi, when, in fact, we are actually repossessing ilandi that was stolen from us by successive unfair governments and uncouth exploitative employers.

M is for (U)Mantshingelane — security guard. There was once a time when being a security guard was every Zulu boy's dream. But then non-Zulus like Nelson Mandela and Mbhazima Shilowa, former premier of Gauteng province, decided to become mantshingelanes. Ah, a great tradition lost its glamour and glory.

N is for (UKU)Nqoba — to be victorious. We love being victorious, no matter what the contest. That's why the ANC had its (siya)nqoba rally after the election.

O is for Ofezela — The Scorpions. Zuma evaded their sting ... just!

P is for (I)Phixiphixi — a hypocrite. The best example of (ama)phixiphixi would be the leaders of Cope (the opposition Congress of the People), who say they are defending the Constitution when, in fact, they served in a regime that undermined it by using state resources to settle political scores. Amaphixiphixi!

Q is for (UKU)Qudula — to be cantankerous. The editor of this paper (The Sunday Times) has his favourite illustration of a person who qudulas — a chief whose surname starts with a B, who is a leader of what once passed itself off as a political party representative of Zulu people.*

R is for... No, we don't have an R in Zulu. We say ilandi, instead of rand, Fled instead of Fred.

S is for (UKU)Shaya — to beat up. But ukushaya is a milder form of beating up. The more appropriate form of beating up is, as we have seen, ukubhaxabula, ukudukluza.

T* is for (AMA)*Tekisi — taxis. We have a monopoly over ibhizinisi yamatekisi (taxi business) — as drivers, queue marshalls, izinkabi (enforcers) and, of course, as owners.

U* is for *Ukudla — food. Who doesn't like it?

V* is for (UKU)*Vova Inkani — to frustrate a person. We derive pleasure from frustrating people. When ANC voters flocked in their numbers to the polling stations in the last election they were collectively determined to do exactly that to the opposition parties – to vova them.

W* is for (UKU)*Wina — we love winning, whether it's a debate, a stick fight, a race between taxis, or the lotto.

X* is for (UKU)*Xoxa — to converse. We like conversing, and we are good raconteurs, as our good president has so ably demonstrated. But X can also be for (uku)xabana — to quarrel. We don't choose to be quarrelsome, it's just that the entire universe is quarrelling with us. So we strike first.

Y* is for *'Yehheni!' — an exclamation of surprise, as in: 'Yehheni-bo! Nansi ingulube inginonela (My golly gosh, this pig is getting fatter)', in other words, 'this person is being quarrelsome with me and I am going to do something to him' (bhibiza him, perhaps.)

Z* is for *Zulu. You know what that means. But Z can also be for (uku)zuma. Ukuzuma is a verb that means 'to ambush', or 'to surprise'. And we all know what Zuma has done — he has surprised many; in other words, he has zuma-ed those who dismissed him as a spent political force given that little matter of the charges.

Now that you've been enlightened about Zulu ways, why not hug that Zulu who's been standing on your stoep begging for your attention? During Mandela's and Mbeki's eras every influential person had his own Indian. Now, every South African must have his or her own Zulu. Continue your zweet interaction with my people!

* Chief Mangosuthu Buthelezi

The Uncle Ernest Stories

Christmas with the Khumalos

AT THE BEGINNING IT WAS JOLLY GOOD FUN, but over the years entertaining members of my extended family — whether they come to my house in Johannesburg or I go to them in my ancestral home in KwaZulu-Natal — has become something of a burden.

The slaughter of the beast has lost its jovial sacredness. The sharing of libations with uncles, aunts and cousins has lost its allure.

As Christmas comes hurtling towards us I can see trouble on the horizon.

That trouble is Uncle Ernest.

There is something enigmatic about maternal uncles. Not only do they tend to be the black sheep in their families, they are also social misfits. I don't know why. Maybe it's the way society looks at them: they are your blood, but are not close enough to have the same surname.

Your father doesn't like them because they invariably tried to stand between him and your mother in the days of courtship.

Or they made him pay huge ilobolo. So, you tend to side with your father in your dislike for your maternal uncles.

Your paternal uncles — obab'omncane — are a different proposition. They are always giving you dirty looks because they think your father is turning you into a spoilt brat; they expect him to be as hard on you as their father was on them. 'Khumalo boys are not supposed to do this, Khumalo boys are not supposed to speak like this ... blah blah blah.' But they are your direct blood; they are Khumalos and you can't do anything about it.

Maternal uncles are almost dispensable, except they stick to you like leeches, especially if you were born out of wedlock.

My earliest recollection of my Uncle Ernest is of an energetic man, flashily dressed, fast-talking, but his mouth devoid of front teeth.

As a boy of five I found it odd that such a big good-looking man had no teeth. I thought toothlessness was the domain of newborn babies, or boys and girls just a year or two older than me, or ancient grandpas and grandmas who had tasted all the food in the world and no longer had any use for teeth.

'He lost his teeth in jail,' my aunts would whisper behind my uncle's back.

Another enigmatic word: jail. What place would deprive you of such important ornaments? How do you eat meat? What do girls say when you smile?

Incidentally, Uncle Ernest was not the only male in our extended family who had just returned from this distant place called jail. My oldest cousin, Mzala Zoo, had also sat alongside uncle in that dark, dank place.

While my uncle came back home with his strength dissipated, Mzala Zoo came back prancing about in a body that was rippling with muscles.

At the time my parents were not yet married and, as is the custom, I was staying with my maternal grandparents in Chesterville, a township just crawling distance from Durban. Uncle Ernest and Mzala Zoo stayed with us — when they were not in jail.

During their stay the two gentlemen used to regale my cousins and me with tales about life in jail.

Mzala Zoo was always telling us how difficult life was there and that we should learn hard at school so that we wouldn't end up entangled in crime, which would lead us to jail. Mzala Zoo was always exercising, shadow-boxing and running up and down the street, in order, he said, to keep fit and healthy — then he would show us the latest boxing moves that he said we should learn if we wanted to be respected on the streets.

There was a twinge of jealousy in the eyes of Uncle Ernest every time we small boys joined Mzala Zoo under the huge avocado tree that stood in the middle of the yard and started shadow-boxing and screaming the fear of God into the heart of an imaginary adversary.

Uncle Ernest would spit derisively into the middle of the yard, his serpentine tongue protruding out of his gap-toothed mouth. He would produce his huge knife and start slashing at an imaginary enemy. Then he would say: 'People in the streets have no time for your boxing shit; they'll slash you like this with their knives while you are jumping about like a poor imitation of Muhammad Ali.'

His moves with the knife were impressive. Kids growing up in the ghetto fall easily under the influence of a man who carries a knife or a gun. There is an aura of glamour and invincibility around him.

Fighting it out with your bare hands is not child's play, as we would later learn when trying to put into practice the moves that Mzala Zoo had tried to impart to us.

We opted for Uncle Ernie's knife-wielding antics. We also liked him because he was talkative and funny, unlike the brooding Mzala Zoo. Serious and sullen people are dangerous because you never know when they are about to snap and give you a klap.

But in the rage of my growing up I began to see Uncle Ernest for what he was: a boisterously troublesome, insecure, attention-seeking brat who was useless without his knife. That is why they punched his teeth out in prison.

A family gathering wouldn't be complete without him causing a scene: either calling my father a country bumpkin or telling all and sundry that his parents had set him up for failure by not sending him to high school — a lie, as he had decided to drop out of school of his own volition in the face of all the caning my grandpa visited upon his skinny ass.

I suppose you are beginning to understand the world of my Uncle Ernie. I suppose you can see why the intimations of Christmas always bring to my mind his name and the things of which he is capable.

I thought that, with age, he would mellow. But not Uncle Ernest.

Not only has he not stopped being a nomad with no fixed abode but, whenever we have a family gathering, he continues to be the centre of attraction — for all the wrong reasons.

When someone threatens him with violence he never forgets to mention that he is a baaaad man: not only has he been to prison many times, he is also a Buthelezi by birth, a clan of warriors you shouldn't mess with. His brother-in-law (referring to my father) is also from the Khumalos, a baaaad clan of warriors. So don't mess with me, my boy. I'm covered.

But if the person threatening him with violence is my father Uncle Ernest just sulks, or he pushes his tongue through the gap between his teeth, points an accusing finger at my father, and shouts: 'Sbali (brother-in-law), you shouldn't be so sure of yourself. Remember you never finished paying ilobolo for my sister. Your kids now have big beards yet you still haven't finished paying ilobolo. A man like you should be the last one to show indiscretion towards his in-laws.'

The one person who could deal effectively with Uncle Ernest, my younger brother Cornelius, has, unfortunately, passed on.

Whenever Uncle Ernest started shouting at people my brother would say: 'Everybody reach for your raincoats! Uncle is going to wet your faces with his waterfall of saliva!' This reference was, of course, to the huge gap between the teeth, which allowed a torrent of saliva to escape from his mouth when he started shouting.

My brother's warning would disarm Uncle Ernest. He would either sulk and walk away, or would succumb to paroxysms of laughter — and then everybody really needed their raincoats.

So, this Christmas I will have to deal with Uncle Ernest single-handedly.

Whenever he starts his antics the older people turn their heads away and pretend he is not there. But to me he is not only a nuisance but a real shame and embarrassment, especially when my in-laws and friends are around. And the bugger knows I would do anything to shut him up.

'Okay, son of my sister,' he will lisp when I start clenching and unclenching my fists in anger. 'Just give a bottle of ugologo obomvu (brandy) and I will leave you in peace so you can sit down with your friends and speak all the English and the politics in the world.'

If Uncle Ernest is insolence personified my paternal aunt Tee works on you like slow poison — by the time you recover from her spell your pockets are dry.

'Awu, mntakabhuti (oh, my brother's child), how about some R200 for your old aunt so she can buy some pantyhose.' The guilt pangs are so intense you part with the money before Tito Mboweni can tell you: 'Tighten your belt.'

No sooner have you given her the money, than you see her dawdling down the streets, her legs buckling under her weight.

'Awu, mntakabhuti, these tsotsis are bad. They have taken all the money you gave to me. How about another R200?'

Everybody in the yard breaks out in laughter for it is clear to all that she is full of beer. Out of pity you give her more notes and she disappears, to look for another victim.

Around New Year she wears a morose face and sings a new tune: 'Awu, mntakabhuti, my kids have to go back to school. Can't you arm me with a handful of rands so I can take care of their stationery.' (This when everybody in the family knows her kids have long dropped out of school.) But her charm still works.

My father's line, during almost every family gathering, is: 'Eish, I wish my soccer team were still around. Look at Patrice Motsepe and Tokyo Sexwale (both enormously wealthy businessmen). Look at their contribution to our soccer. If only I had a hotline to one of them. Perhaps they would help me resuscitate my team.'

You see, when I was a boy, he owned a soccer team which did relatively well, ending up in the second division of the then National Professional Soccer League.

In his heart of hearts he thinks I have enough money to help him claw back the enchanted past and, from the dustbins of history, yank out his dream of being at the helm of a soccer team.

I don't know why I do this to myself, but I find myself salivating at the prospect of this year's gathering of the clan.

At the beginning of this piece I mused on the fact that maternal uncles are strange characters.

Now I wonder what my sisters' children make of me. I will start watching them closely this coming Christmas. Maybe they even have a nickname for me. Maybe they think I'm too stingy, or too aloof, or too much in love with the waters of immortality…

To be a maternal uncle is definitely not child's play. I'm beginning to love Uncle Ernest all over again, and to look forward to his Christmas crap.

21 Decemder 2005

The lady with the knife

WOMEN. I LOVE THEM; SOMETIMES I HATE THEM. Sometimes they scare me to death; other times they invoke in me such deep, inexplicable emotions that I feel my eyes getting misty and my knees turning to jelly.

In my long life I have encountered different types of women: those with eyes that seem to be looking into the distance, to an elusive future where they will at last achieve lasting peace, far from their current, unbearable circumstances. These types make me sad; they make me feel bad to be a man, a creature whose mission in life is to break the hearts of women who need to be loved and treasured.

But then I've encountered some women with aggressive, ready-to-fight demeanours; women who make you feel like an endangered species; ball-busters; women with faces as stark as those of hunting dogs – gashes across them, strong jaws and mean determined eyes, unflinching under all circumstances.

Let me tell you about one woman who left an impression on me from a young age, a lady who remains an iconic presence in my mind – a woman who has influenced, in one way or the other, the way I perceive women and relate to them. I will paint the picture, and hope you are visionary enough to reach your own conclusions about her, to pass your own judgement, if need be.

Sis Makho was a shark of a woman. She left a trail of blood wherever she went. The blood could be from men who would stab and kill each other for her attention, or it could be the blood of an obstinate but foolish Romeo who underestimated Sis Makho's ability and speed with her knife.

Sis Makho carried two knives on her person, one in her handbag, another at her 'dairy', as a woman's cleavage used to be called in the street argot of the time. And she never hesitated to use her knife, on both male and female offenders.

A light-complexioned vixen with sparkling eyes, she had an artificial gap between her top front teeth, as was the fashion at the time. Short of stature, she was bow-legged in a seductive, Halle Berry way.

I must have been six or seven when I first met Sis Makho. But even then, before the ravages of time and experience taught me a thing or two about women and their breasts, I couldn't help noticing that hers were bigger than normal. And she seemed to thrust them forward as she sashayed down the street in her high-heeled shoes.

Upon her appearance on the street a group of boisterous men playing cards or throwing dice would suddenly fall silent – as if an angel was passing, as we used to say. With the benefit of hindsight, I think I can picture the denizens of the street getting cross-eyed as they ogled Sis Makho's gazoongas, as breasts were called then.

Like a shark Sis Makho always and only moved forward. That is until she encountered my mother's younger brother, Uncle Ernest.

It's not that Uncle Ernest tamed Sis Makho, or anything of the sort. It's just that he, unlike the other men whose hearts she had broken, managed to slow her down. He came to the point of almost owning her. But strong-willed as he was and feared as he was in the streets – he was fast and accurate with his knife – Uncle Ernest could not own Sis Makho. Nobody could.

He made a common law wife of her, to the envy of an army of men who would have done anything – including kill each other – to have their names carved into Sis Makho's heart. When she moved in with us Sis Makho became the centrepiece of our big family. Because my parents were not yet married I lived with my maternal grandparents at their Chesterville house, alongside other brats who were my cousins – sons and daughters of my mother's elder sisters.

Sis Makho – when she felt like – cooked for the entire family. But when she didn't feel like, she only cooked for herself and her boyfriend, Uncle Ernest.

Sis Makho and Uncle Ernest kept very irregular hours. While all the big people were at work during the week the two would loiter about the yard, smoking cigarette after cigarette, and sometimes drinking beer. But they were moderate in their drinking during the week because, when the other big people came back from work Uncle Ernest and Sis Makho would get dressed in their smart clothes and take a bus to the city. That's where they worked.

For some time I couldn't understand why granny used to curse the two almost every time they left for work: 'One slinyana day, nina nobabili niyowukhomba umuzi onotshwala – one foolish day, you two will regret what you are doing, behaving like bed bugs that live on other people's blood.'

To a six-year-old boy such words were a riddle. It was much later that I learned that Sis Makho and Uncle Ernest were feared pickpockets in the city. When they got desperate, they would simply mug you. But even if they had to mug you, violence was their last resort.

Unlike other pickpockets, who moved in groups of five or six or more and would descend on their prey like hungry wolves, Uncle Ernest and Sis Makho operated on their own. Always well dressed, Sis Makho would use her charm to attract an unsuspecting Romeo to come close to her. When the two started getting amorous – before the days of sexual harassment charges men were quick to touch a woman – Uncle Ernest would appear out of nowhere and create a huge scene, accusing the unsuspecting Romeo of stealing money from his wife. Uncle Ernest would start beating up the poor guy while emptying his pockets.

Or Makho would turn on her charm, luring the man into a quiet alley, only to have Uncle Ernest appear out of nowhere to pounce with a vengeance on the poor joe.

While my grandma, MaSibisi, disapproved of their nocturnal escapades, she enjoyed it when the couple came home groaning under the weight of plastic bags of groceries. They would treat her to boxes of snuff, and would sometimes even buy her beer.

There seemed to be a love-hate relationship between MaSibisi and Sis Makho, her makoti. She strongly disapproved of her criminal escapades and blamed her own son's wayward behaviour on her. Mothers will always be mothers, tenaciously protective and blaming the entire world for the unfortunate behaviour of their offspring.

There were times when Uncle Ernest and Sis Makho had loud fights; beer bottles were thrown, knives were produced, but they never reached the point of actually using the knives on each other. It was whispered in the house that on the nights when the two were at loggerheads Uncle Ernest would sleep with one eye open and his knife under his pillow. Uncle Ernest would later tell me how scared he was of dying under a woman's knife. A contemporary of his, a serial killer by the name of Qhogola, after all the countless people who had fallen before his own knife, suffered just such a fate.

What a shame, Uncle Ernest would sneer; what a dirty shame, for ulova to die under a woman's blade!

Whenever they fought, MaSibisi would threaten to chase Uncle Ernest and Sis Makho out of her house.

But when MaSibisi was happy – after a couple of cartons of sorghum beer – she would engage her makoti in long, friendly chatter. Years later I would learn that the older woman saw a younger version of herself in this tough-as-nails makoti of hers. MaSibisi had been born in one of the shantytowns of Pretoria and could speak hardcore

Afrikaans. She could also speak tsotsitaal, Pretoria style, which she would display to her children and grandchildren when the waters of immortality got the better of her. She had apparently been something of a wayward child growing up in Pretoria. Her parents decided to take her to relatives in Ladysmith, where she spent her teenage years.

She later married Mkhulu Buthelezi, my mother's father, who was, at some stage, a lay preacher.

By the mid-to-late 1970s my parents had gotten married and my mother left her parents' house, to move with her new family to a township called Mpumalanga near the industrial town of Hammarsdale in the Natal Midlands.

It was during that time that Uncle Ernest was thrown in prison for a long time. In his life, prison had always been his second home, but this spell seemed very long indeed. By that time I had more important things to think about and laugh at than the antics of Uncle Ernest and the makoti he never got around to marrying. I took pride in the fact that my parents were now married and therefore had no truck with people who viewed the institution of marriage with disdain.

This attitude had been instilled in me, no doubt, by my mother, who was very strict, always talking about the importance of education in helping people achieve stability in their lives: have a good job, start a family and achieve stability – 'unlike the likes of your uncle and that woman of his!' The last sentence was spat out with regret and bitterness.

With mum assuming this kind of attitude it was therefore natural for me to jettison Sis Makho and Uncle Ernest in River Lethe, the river in which we dump all that should be forgotten in life as we know it.

When Uncle Ernest was arrested Sis Makho abandoned my grandma's house and went back to wherever she'd come from. But with the news of Uncle Ernest's return she suddenly reappeared, a long-missed phantom. By that time Uncle Ernest was older and wiser. His former friends and fellow criminals had either died, or moved on to bigger things: selling drugs or robbing banks.

Such missions had violence on a larger scale written all over them. I don't think Uncle Ernest was ready to venture into the big league. He never was an overtly violent criminal; he only stabbed when he had been pushed into a corner. Even then, he did not stab to kill but to get people out of the way. On his release this time around, it seemed that he was no longer prepared to revert to pickpocketing and mugging, but he still had to earn a living. With no education or any skills that could see him gainfully employed, he was at a loss as to how to proceed. Besides, pickpocketing had become a bit of a challenge, what with the streets of Durban awash with police. A plan had to be made.

It was Sis Makho who came up with the plan. The couple embarked on a new scheme … or scam, if you will.

Instead of leaving the house at nightfall as they had done in the past, Uncle Ernest and Sis Makho began to leave in the morning, like all gainfully employed adults. What they did wherever they went to during the day remained a mystery to many for a long time. They certainly were not picking pockets or the family would have been apprised of that by neighbours who made other people's affairs their own. Remarkably, they each carried a huge sports bag stuffed with whatever it was. At the end of each day, they would come back home with wads of money.

It was only much later that we learnt what they were up to.

Issue 6 Vol 1, August/ September 2008. Afropolitan Magazine.

The return of the prodigal Zulu son

WHEN I WAS OF SCHOOL-GOING AGE the beginning of a new year was a time for both New Year's resolutions and report-backs.

Report-backs to friends about how you spent the festive season, but also report-backs to teachers, who would ask you to write about your journey to the rural areas.

The insinuation, of course, being that black people did not belong in the city, or its outskirts, but in some back-of-beyond homeland. Ah, Verwoerd did well!

Some of us, of course, were born and bred in the townships.

My father, who was born in Ixopo, had no reason to visit his place of birth frequently as there was simply nothing to do back there.

So we stayed in the township during the festive season, or at least visited my mother's place of birth - - which was yet another township, Chesterville.

When our language teachers demanded of us a composition about our visits to our 'ancestral homelands', many of us had to take refuge in creative writing.

I had to create romantic journeys to some faraway kingdom where my father was revered and treated like a prince, where food was plentiful, where clear streams gurgled with clean water, where the cattle were fat and healthy, thanks to the verdant blankets of green grass covering the undulating hills of our land (yes, that was the style admired by the teachers).

Anyway, I am back from my Christmas break.

But I have no romantic tales to tell. Gritty tales of the hard life of the townships are all I have for you.

Long-lost childhood friends who have become old men with no teeth, childhood girlfriends who now look like grannies; these are the sights that confronted me when I visited the township of my childhood.

When you ask, 'Where is so and so? ' they look at you with incredulity. Immediately you know the one after whose health you've just asked has passed on.

The main cause of death lingers on the lips of the speakers ... unspoken. Ask no more.

But beyond the gritty scenes, I have some tender tales as well.

When my younger brother got married three days before Christmas, the family slaughtered two fat cows as part of the feast. And a goat.

There was no talk of cholesterol or concerns about obesity as we sank our teeth into succulent pieces of the freshly slaughtered beasts.

Everyone from our part of the township came and gathered under the marquee. When that was too full, others sheltered around our house, while still others, too drunk to have any common sense at all, collapsed under the sweltering heat of the KwaZulu-Natal sun. You don't invite people to these feasts; they just come.

And my Uncle Ernest was there. Because he is one of those who tend to perform to a gallery, threatening all and sundry with violence of epic proportions at the slightest provocation, I was concerned that he would start causing scenes.

In between my chores as the Main Man in charge of logistics, I plied Uncle Ernest with glass after glass from my choice of whiskies.

As he succumbed to the potency of the whisky he started waxing lyrical about his prowess, in days gone by, with the knife. He told how well-known gangsters of Chesterville, such as Qhogola, used to shiver at the sight of him.

Over our sniggers at his tales of gallantry were ladled huge dollops of disbelief and dismissiveness.

That was until one of my cousins, much older than me, a sober-minded fellow who spent more time with Uncle Ernest than any of us, started bearing testimony to how Qhogola would wilt in fear at the mere appearance of Uncle Ernest.

Upon release from an umpteenth spell in prison — sans front teeth — Uncle Ernest told us he started working as a fortune teller on Grey Street in Durban, beguiling people into parting with their pay cheques.

'I wasn't using my knife any more,' he said, guffawing, 'I was using my brains and my charm, telling them to close their eyes while I laid my hands on their wallets and prayed for the protection of their money from wily tsotsis. By the time they opened their eyes I would have stolen their money from them and stuffed the wallet with pieces of paper. I would tell them not to open their wallets until they got home. And they obeyed.'

What amazes me is that this scam, called Isalamusi, was perfected back in the '70s, but people, to this day, are still falling for it.

Uncle Ernest is no longer an operator, but there are many of them in Durban and Johannesburg (I'm not sure about Cape Town).

Anyway, the day after the wedding, Uncle Ernest went to his house. My newly wed brother and I joined him there on Christmas day. More feasting. Then we drove to Chesterville, my township of birth, for more eating and drinking.

I had brought a couple of bottles of good whisky. Again, Uncle Ernest plunged into it with alacrity. Now we were sitting with his peers, people who had been there when he was carrying out his scams. As the booze took its toll on him and his friends the language started getting stronger. I expected trouble any moment, having seen that Uncle Ernest was carrying his ubiquitous knife.

But I sighed in relief when, at the end of the day, he was still standing and there had been no violence.

'You surprised me, uncle, this time,' I said, as my teetotaller younger brother drove us home, 'You didn't get into any fights.'

Without batting an eyelid, Uncle Ernest said: 'Fighting is expensive these days. Besides, you boys made me drink some expensive liquor today. Expensive liquor doesn't get you drunk like your usual cheap shit – Smirnoff and the like.'

He paused. 'Yeah, if you want to keep me on the straight and narrow, keep buying me that expensive shit ... it's good for my sanity, and it's good for the safety of those around me, hahaha!'

Uncle Ernest is one of those raconteurs who can keep you spellbound for a whole day with stories so colourful and dramatic you'd think they had sprouted from a fertile imagination.

Only when you get people to corroborate these fantastic stories independently do you begin to appreciate the fragility of the times in which he and his peers grew up. There's a book to be written somewhere there.

The last leg of my journey in the great kingdom took me to Ulundi, where one of my friends was getting married.

Once again, we had to eat lots of meat. The bugger slaughtered three cattle and I don't know how many goats. But, by this time, my stomach was toyi-toying furiously.

I had to run to the toilet every now and then, and somebody sniggered that my stomach had become used to 'weak' food — prawns and stuff — and could no longer handle proper food: meat, meat and more meat.

So, neighbours and friends, the Zulu boy is back, still nursing a very angry stomach.

When I had a green salad for lunch the other day, the editor made it a point to share this morsel of news with everyone in the office. He is Zulu, you see, and thinks I am letting the side down.

How can a proud descendant of Mageba and Mzilikazi start competing with rabbits and cattle for leaves and other 'lousy' food? What a shame.

Celery anyone?

6 Janaury 2008

In A Manner Of Speaking

The knobkerrie knoweth not the English language

THE ONE REMARKABLE THING OUR GAUTENG PREMIER, Mbhazima Sam Shilowa, did was to leave his job as a security guard in good time.

He then proceeded to become the general secretary of the Congress of South African Trade Unions (and they say bad, lazy workers make good unionists).

Anyway, having resigned as a security guard, Shilowa acquired a taste for good whisky and cigars. His dress sense also improved — except for the red socks to which he still clings.

But we are not sitting here talking about Shilowa's dress sense per se — what we are trying to explore is a new development in the security industry.

Now, being a security guard is not for sissies, what with every next man and his dog running crazy with AK-47s and 9mm pistols. This is a job for tough guys.

With global warming (whatever that means) this country has become so cold in winter that places that have not seen snow in a long time, if ever, have experienced the white stuff over the past few weeks. I include parts of Johannesburg in this. Imagine yourself being a security guard, standing out there in the cold, being irritated not only by the ferocious wind biting your face, but also by the cold customers who refuse to roll down their windows and sign the register as they enter your employer's premises.

It's a tough job this, only good for Zulus, who are known for their patience (some say stubbornness). It is also because of their stubbornness that Zulus make good taxi drivers. Yes, you have to be lugubrious in demeanour and temperament to make it as a security guard — if they don't kill you on the job. It is not surprising that the recent labour strike by security guards was one of the most violent in recent memory. Good security guards can be matched only by taxi drivers in their talent for driving fear into the hearts of ordinary human beings.

Only a taxi driver can talk on the cellphone, drive, sing praises to his car, collect fares from his passengers and swear at them — all at the same time. 'Ubani ongakhokhanga? Ohho, yehlikani nonke emotweni yami (Who hasn't paid? All right, you get out of my car, all of you!).' Screech! He brings his car to a halt and produces a knobkerrie.

And only in Zulu (and possibly in Afrikaans) can you swear in a manner that drives the fear of God into your adversary's heart.

English-speaking people (and I mean real English people, not these pommies we have in South Africa) are so prim and proper you'd think they were reciting a poem in your honour when they are trying to insult you. Bill Cosby says the English are so uptight and they stand straight as a rod, and when they are collapsing and dying they will apologise: 'I'm so embarrassed that I'm leaning, but seeing that life is leaving me ...'

Many of my friends are Tswana-speaking, but every time they insult me I just raise my Zulu eyebrows and shrug my Zulu shoulders, because their insults lack the venom that an insult is supposed to carry.

And I've been told that Swazis, because they can't fight, use only insults as their weapon against approaching marauders. But I just laugh when my Swazi friend swears at me because all those sibilant tones in his language make it sound as if he is proposing love to me. 'Sibatfukile, wena mlomo longacali manga (We insulted them, You Mouth Which Doesn't Tell Lies)'*

Now, where was I? Ah, talking about security guards, and their new set of problems.

Last week I read a report in Ilanga, a Zulu-language newspaper, that a company called Royal Security has come up with a very worrisome edict aimed at security guards.

The company has decided that a security guard who is late for work will forfeit a day's salary and also be penalised R200. If a security guard is found sleeping on the job, he will be penalised R300.

But — and this is what is important — every time a security guard 'breaks' the English language, he will be penalised R100. Hhayi bo!

Now why would you want a security guard to speak impeccable English? I agree it's important that he or she be able to communicate in the language — so he can tell the robbers where the baas's safe is situated — but he doesn't have to be a Charles Dickens.

The more inarticulate in the language, the better, and the more unlikely he is to co-operate with today's robbers, who, I hear, speak impeccable English ('What's the combination to your boss's safe, motherf***er?' and 'Where's your madam's jewellery box, asshole?')

A security guard who is inarticulate in English is a better proposition because he will not wax lyrical about the intricacies of the layout of the house and the nooks and crannies the robber will have to negotiate to get to valuable goods.

Seriously, don't force these security guards to speak immaculate English, otherwise they will spend time asking themselves questions such as 'to be or not to be?' while the robbers are busy helping themselves to the employers' belongings.

The other danger is that once they learn to speak good English they will forget about their work and hanker after all the good things that their former colleague, Mbhazima Shilowa, is enjoying. We need security guards who make the knobkerrie do the talking, and the knobkerrie speaks only one language. Ehhe!

*In Nguni languages such as isiZulu and siSwati the king is called the Mouth Which Doesn't Tell Lies, in other words, he is beyond reproach.

20 August 2006

English is killing Julius Malema

IT WONDERS ME WHY JULIUS MALEMA, that contumelious president of the
African National Congress Youth League, still insists on using public platforms to speak
English, a language that clearly defeats his intellect.

Okay, you purists out there, before you reach for your shotguns and punish me for
what looks like a grammatically wrong opening sentence, in fact that sentence is per-
fectly acceptable in Pennsylvania, where they speak an English called Pennsylvania
Dutch, which adapts English phrases to Germanic syntax and idiom.

I chose to open this column in this bizarre fashion to draw readers' attention to the
vagaries of the English language as she is spoken — and broken — all over the world.

I've lived and worked with native English speakers for a long time, not only in this
country but in North America as well, and even these native speakers admit that English
is a gargantuan animal that needs to be handled with care.

My friend Jacob Dlamini has written an online article in which he makes some
interesting remarks about English as she is masticated by my fellow countrymen.

He writes: 'As a colleague at Business Day once pointed out to me, only in South
Africa would people use the word shame when a baby is born ('Shame, what a beautiful
baby'); when that baby falls and hurts itself ('Shame, poor thing!') and when that baby
dies ('Ag shame, what a shame!').

But that's just South Africa.

Why would you differ with a Martian who's just landed on Earth and is logically
suggesting that the opposite of overwhelm should be 'underwhelm'? What, indeed,
does 'whelm' mean? How do you do it?

We say: 'I did something in one fell swoop', but what is meant by 'fell'?

In English, shove doesn't rhyme with move. Though the plural of mouse is mice, you
would be crucified if you were to suggest that the plural of house should, therefore,
be hice!

Try to explain the word 'the' to a Martian and let's see how far you get.

You will recall that I invoked the name of one Julius Malema at the beginning of this
column. I had no intention of writing about him.

All I meant to write about was the intricacies of the Queen's tongue, the vagaries
of this language we love so much.

It just so happens that Malema is the fly that continues to find itself in this English ointment.

Not so long ago the man-who-was-dropped-on-his-head when he was small made his now infamous statement that he and his comrades would kill for Zuma.

When critics expressed outrage at this language of incitement he was at pains to explain that the context had been misunderstood, that he had not meant kill as in kill, as in robbing a person of his life.

He had meant kill in another sense, a sense that was not successfully explained to us. But, tolerant citizens that we are, we let it ride. Maybe he meant kiss? Now that would have been very desirable — 'we will kiss in the name of the revolution'. 'Make love, not war,' the hippies used to say.

Now, again, Malema is back in the news — not for some courageous act or for his benevolence to the nation: no, he is again in a jam as a result of the English language.

Malema said on Sunday that as South Africa readied itself for next year's elections* that questions needed to be asked about how service delivery could be accelerated, and poverty halved, by 2014.

'We must also intensify the struggle to eliminate the remnants of counter-revoltion, which include the DA and a loose coalition of those who want to use state power to block the ANC president's ascendancy to the highest office of the land.'

There has been a brouhaha about Malema's choice of words — especially the word 'eliminate', which was interpreted by many to mean 'kill'. Malema has denied that it was his intention to use the word 'eliminate' to mean that. He said that by eliminate he had meant 'remove'.

Incidentally, those of us who were around during the apartheid years will recall that Adrian Vlok's people used the expression 'remove from society' to mean 'kill', eliminate. That was well documented by the Truth and Reconciliation Commission.

In the ensuing debate about the appropriateness of the word 'eliminate' some people suggested Malema should have used his home language to explain himself. While Malema was still considering that, one of his comrades, a top official in the Youth League, volunteered a word in an SMS to a colleague: eliminate (ukususa).

Those who speak Zulu will tell you that the language of King Shaka is very shy on euphemisms and ambiguities: ukususa is a very strong word that carries the same meaning as 'to remove permanently from society'. It's a chilling word.

I therefore implore Malema, in his future public addresses, to use his home language, or an unambiguous Zulu word or expression, to avoid being misunderstood.

It seems that English tends to refuse to communicate accurately what he has on his mind; it is a language with a will of its own. It needs people who are intellectually tenacious and are willing to take ownership of it and tame it to do what they want to do with it. It's a cruel language, this English. It therefore wonders me why Malema has not come to this realisation.

*The elections were held on 22 April 2009.

20 July 2008

French leaves le Zoulou blank

TO A SELF-RESPECTING, fashion-conscious South African there is nothing as debilitating and completely dispiriting as finding yourself in a foreign country dressed in an oversized, uncomfortable collection of rags, and a scarf that makes you look like a ninja — all in the name of protecting yourself from the cold.

And yet that's exactly what I am experiencing now, in the first few days of my sojourn in Saint-Nazaire, a town on the north-western coast of France.

When I arrived here, resplendent in my fancy leather jacket, jeans and takkies, I must have looked like a sad clown to the locals because the mercury was hovering around -4ºC; the following day, conditions had improved immensely — the thermometer was recording a 'summery' 2ºC.

Let me hasten to add that I had been warned about the cold by those who are familiar with French winters, but having been to this country before, albeit in the middle of July, the height of summer, I thought I could imagine what winters here could be like. Wrong.

Anyway, when I arrived, my hosts took one look at my clothes, shook their heads ruefully and advised me to go and get myself something warmer before I froze to death. They also gave me my per diem so I could buy some groceries.

That brought me to hurdle number two: the language. Back home I can move around easily as I speak English, Zulu, Xhosa and Afrikaans, and can have what passes for a decent conversation in most of the other languages.

But here, in the middle of small-town France, the smattering of French I thought I knew disappeared under the unforgiving faces of French people, who are absolutely unperturbed that they can't speak English — and they expect you to pronounce at least some of their words correctly. Try to pronounce this: six oeufs biologiques de poules. Now try it in English: six chicken eggs. In Zulu: amaqanda enkukhu ayisithupha.

Well, when in France, do as Asterix would have done. Imagine, then, me trying to buy some groceries at the local store. I found myself sounding like a four-year-old, or some intellectually retarded person speaking in nouns and broken phrases: lait, bovine, legumes, (milk, beef, vegetables). Moi, écrivain (Me, a writer.) Afrique du Sud, oui (South Africa, yes.)

Given time, I can write some pretty impressive sentences in French. Okay, half-decent ones.

The problem is that you don't have the luxury of time when you are queueing for service at a shop. Secondly, all the beautiful French words that I can write are almost impossible for an English-speaking person who has never lived with French speakers to pronounce.

Come to think of it, English is not even my first language. Thanks to apartheid education, I am largely self-taught when it comes to the language. Many of our teachers could write beautiful words in English, but when it came to pronunciation it became an uphill struggle for both teacher and pupil.

Many of us were taught by teachers who made the word 'scathing' rhyme with 'scatting', and 'determine' to rhyme with 'undermine'.

Understandably, they'd never been exposed to conversational English. When a black person interacted with a white person, it was usually to receive instructions.

Now, I cannot imagine a white South African using elegant English to give instrutions to his gardener: 'John, I am determined that you rid my lovely lawn of the dog's repugnant excretion.'

I think the white baas would have said something like: 'John, clean dog moosh-moosh.'

Anyway, having used sign language and French Fanagalo to buy my groceries, I went back to my apartment. Ah, a well-appointed abode it is. In summer, looking out of the window from this tenth-floor apartment must be splendid, giving you a panoramic sweep of the port of Saint-Nazaire and the Atlantic. But right now, one look at the expanse of water simply makes my bum freeze.

The worst of my linguistic challenges was yet to come. Later that day I realised that one of my computer cables was not compatible with the wall plugs here. I scratched my head and looked at my French phrase book trying to figure out how I was to explain my predicament. I ended up hauling my laptop to the computer shop.

When I finally got there, I had to take the computer out of its case and show the salesman the cable connections. Thankfully, he wasn't dumb, but I definitely looked it as I gesticulated, pointing at the computer and cables, wringing my hands to show that I was pleading for his assistance. The whole experience was a study in frustration and embarrassment.

Travelling humbles you.

Before I left home, my wife encouraged me to take some French lessons. I did a perfunctory job of it, confident that the few phrases of French I knew would enable me to get by in France.

I also reminded my wife that this would not be my first visit to the land of Camus and Sartre, whose work I have devoured — in English, of course.

What I forgot was that during my first visit there I had an official translator who opened many doors for me that would have remained closed as a result of my inability to speak the language.

Now, I wanted to share with you some of the pictures of myself in my bizarre clothing. The problem is that my camera is playing tricks on me and I can't download my pictures to my computer. Solution? I have to go to that computer shop again. Nope, won't be going there in a hurry. One can take only so much punishment in the embarrassment stakes.

Au revoir.

11 January 2009

Yo, Niggas, whaz happenin' to da English?

ALTHOUGH WE HAVE THIS LOVE-HATE RELATIONSHIP WITH THE AMERICANS — thanks to what we perceive as their arrogance and their jingoistic tendencies — we at least understand the language they speak.

In fact, one of my friends says he will defend US imperialism with his life — because he can't imagine himself being colonised by the Chinese.

'I spent almost my entire life trying to learn and understand the intricacies of English,' he says.

'I cannot, therefore, for the life of me, even begin to imagine myself trying to learn Mandarin, or whatever dialect the mainland Chinese will foist upon us once they've conquered us. Let's defend the Americans with our lives.'

I think my friend has a point, even though he tends to overstretch it.

We love the English language, yes, but I wouldn't go so far as to die for a nation that harbours characters who mistake me for a caveman whenever I go there and mention that I am from Africa.

Besides, the Americans do not speak good English, hahaha. Otherwise Bill Cosby wouldn't be so mad at them, especially his black brethren and the brand of English they call Ebonics (from ebony and phonics, see?).

Cosby once railed: 'They are standing on the corner and they can't speak English. I can't even talk the way these people talk: why you ain't, where you is, what he drive, where he say, where he work, who you be ... And I blamed the kid until I heard the mother talk. And then I heard the father talk.

'Everybody knows it's important to speak English, except these knuckleheads. You can't be a doctor with that kind of crap coming out of your mouth.

'In fact, you will never get any kind of job making a decent living. People marched and were hit in the face with rocks to get an education, and now we've got these knuckleheads walking around.'

Look, I do realise the debate on Ebonics, or black American English, is as old as slavery itself, but it keeps coming up.

The likes of Cosby are advocating that, although they understand that every language has slang, there is no need to elevate Ebonics to a language.

This assertion came in the wake of a decision by the Oakland School Board in December 1996 to recognise Ebonics as the primary language of African-American students and to use it in schools.

I am raising the issue of Ebonics because this brand of what I call broken English is gaining currency among our young people.

Listen to the radio and you are bound to hear some airhead who thinks he is 'cool' saying some mind-numbing hogwash such as: 'Yo, my niggas, thingz waz happenin' at Proverb's pardee at da weekend, you know.'

It's so sad that we want to copy everything American and, in many instances, do not even understand the background thereof.

Like many detractors of Ebonics Cosby says this brand of English is plain lazy and makes a mockery of the struggles that black Americans waged so that their children and generations thereafter could get a proper education.

The argument put forward by those who wanted Ebonics to be part of the teaching curriculum was that because black Americans generally speak this brand of English at home it makes sense for them to be taught in the same vernacular at school so they are able to grasp proper English. To me, a product of Bantu Education, this sounds sadly   familiar. Our teachers of English were so poor in the language that they spoke to us in Zulu in order to teach us English. Which is why many of us still speak English based on Zulu or Setswana grammar and speech patterns. 'Ngizwa iphunga (I hear a smell).' But of course, that was because we were given a poor education. In a normalised environment — where everyone has access to the same education — surely that shouldn't happen? We should all strive for standard English. I am, of course, a snob, forgive me, but that's my take on this. Here are some samples of Ebonics as she is spoken in da American 'hoods: Ebonics: 'Yo G, you frontin' me?' English: 'Excuse me, my peer, are you attempting to influence me to engage in violent action with you?' Ebonics: 'You gots to git those Benjamins so you cin git dat bling-bling fo yo ride.' English: 'You must get money so that you can get expensive accessories for your car.' Ebonics: 'Sheeeeiit, foo, I'z be doin' dat shit an' shorty be axin me fo sum scrilla.' English: 'Shit, friend, I am doing that stuff and my girlfriend is asking me for some money.' Fred: 'Yo G, it take me a lifetime to learn dat shit. Leave my standard English alone.'

2 December 2007

What Bantu Education Taught Me ... Not

'I GOT FOKOL FROM BANTU EDUCATION,' the ANC chief whip in the Mpumalanga legislature, Jackson Mthembu, railed at his colleagues recently, sending the DA chihuahuas scurrying for their pens and papers so they could write to the media about what they termed 'unparliamentary' speech.

Bantu Education, you see, thanks to Verwoerd, the founding father of the apartheid system, was meant to prepare us blacks to be manual labourers. Those of us who hate using their hands and strength to earn a living decided that they would become intellectuals (that was before the controversial writer Ronald Suresh Roberts introduced the 'native' prefix to this epithet. Come to think of it, we never imagined that we would be blessed with the great RSR's intellectual interventions a few decades later.)

To be a good intellectual, when you are not dispensing invective, you have to be able to write well.

To hone our writing skills, we used to put a lot of creative energy into our letters to would-be lovers.

Here are some samples: 'Dear Sugar: Time and ability plus double capacity has forced my pen to dance automatically on this benedicted sheet of paper. Why this miraculous thing happened is because, Papie, I love you spontaneously and as I stand horizontal to the wall and perpendicular to the ground I only think of you, since you are a fantastic and fabulous guy. Stop haranguing with the feelings in my heart because I love you more than a snake loves the rat. Each time I see you, my metabolism stops and my peristalsis goes in reverse gear. My medulla oblongata also stops functioning.

'I think I have to pen-off here because I still haven't finished studying. Sleep tight and don't let those bed bugs ever bite you coz you are too sweet a thing for them.

'Yourz Ever, Sugar nonoza'

The boyfriend writes back: 'Dear Honie, i was exasperated with pride to have received one from you, the lungs in my body flapped with joy when i have been reading your letter. Anyway by now you have reached the realisations to why i am jotting this small letter to you, yes it is to see if you are keeping with the sands of time.

'How is everything on that side of yours? Well here everything is just half lemon half sugar to make it Schweppes. How is your schooling? How are you pulling the wagons of life?

'If words of love could ride a bicycle I would be competing against Diego Maradona. Anyways, i will not stop you from reading the books that give you life and education so i will stop here for today. Please always writing to me because i am missing you like sugar misses tea.

'Yours in flesh and in blood, Ruise Sugar Baby. PS Sorry about my english, i did not learn anymore. [Fred whispers: The guy stopped his schooling so he could work at a factory so he could buy her Ambi and other skin-lightening creams.]'

But check this guy out: 'Salutations from the love-hungry horizons:

'I hope this missive finds you in the best of healths. I hope you are still inhaling and exhaling in this globosity. I hope the chlorophyll of life is supplying fresh oxygenous air to your precious lungs. I am collapsing at the doors of desperation now. I have been knocking at the door of your heart but you won't let me in.

'Just let me in and you will see because by so doing you will force me to buy you a aeroplane for you, but if the white government doesn't allow a black person to buy an aeroplane, I will buy you a train ... and if that fails, ag, a taxi will do ... but just for the two of us only and not all the tramps of the unwashed streets.'

And then a scorned girl:

'Dear Prospective Father of My Childrens, What is this I hear through the grapevines of the township? Even the dogs are laughing at the futility of my efforts at showing my deep affection to you. I have always thought you and me were like the tongue and the saliva. Now, it's like we are the east and west, like Mandela and Botha. You have taken my heart and are running away with it.

'But no, you are not caressing my very heart with the romantic hands of love as you promised when we sat and ate fish and chiefs at KwaMagaba the other afternoon.

'You are tearing my heart into veritable shreds of betrayal as you have been seen walking hand in hand, hip to hip with that squinty-eyed girl from down your street. Bring back my heart so I can sew it back into my bosom, the very bosom you once said you will never forsake.'

The boy would respond cruelly: 'Our golden cup is broken. We're finito.'

Our Model C kids, with their emaciated imagination and anaemic vocab, can only write on their cellphones: 'ws gr8 bng wt u. lv u. c u l8r alig8r.' Cry, the beloved country, cry for the loss of expressive language.

And that moegoe politician from Mamparalanga still maintains he got fokol from Bantu Education!

Bantu Education armed him with the ability to be brave with language, to do literal translations from his native tongue into English without seeing anything wrong — that's how he could say fokol in the legislature and shrug his shoulders in bemusement when the chihuahuas complained.

15 July 2007

Race To The Finish

So this Shangaan walks into a rooinek bar ...

WHENEVER A WAITER GIVES HIM A HALF-FULL GLASS OF WINE a friend of mine always retorts: 'Man, fill this glass up. My nose won't drown in the wine. I am not a white man.'

I don't mind when he makes the remark to a black waiter, even in the presence of our white friends, or, indeed, in the presence of his wife, who is of the Caucasian persuasion.

But I do get worried when he makes the remark in the presence of white strangers, who might mistake him for a humourless racist.

In a racially sensitive country such as ours, one does need to be careful about the kind of ethnic jokes/remarks that one makes.

The case of a guy in Klerksdorp last weekend who allegedly killed another who called him a Shangaan is instructive.

Over the years, and because they are in the minority, Shangaans have been the butt of many bad jokes. It's been said they are stupid and have no fashion sense (they are said to wear green shirts, yellow trousers and red shoes). An inferior form of polony/sausage sold in the townships is called Shangaan wors.

Therefore, if a person calls you a Shangaan, it's considered the height of insolence — especially if you are not a Shangaan.

Ethnic stereotypes are not the preserve of black socialisation. English and Afrikaans people have stereotypical barbs they use on each other: rooinek, rock spider, limey, pommy ...

In the case of black South Africa, with the possible exception of those in Johannesburg, which has always been a melting pot, black people from different ethnic groups didn't know each other's languages and cultures.

This lack of understanding, therefore, became a breeding ground for many acerbic ethnic insults and stereotypes.

Zulus were dismissed as warlike and stupid. Sothos were cowards who spied on their black brethren on behalf of white bosses. Tswanas were stingy and mean-spirited (they'd rather drown themselves than give the enemy the pleasure of beating them up).

Vendas were thick headed but well endowed. Historically, Swazis couldn't fight to save their lives; all they could do was insult their enemies and hope the latter would wither away under the immense power of the insults.

Friday was known as Boesman's Christmas because of the perception that coloured people spent their money on delicacies and booze come Friday, payday, and were dirt poor by Monday.

When Zulu people want to tell you how inebriated you are they say: 'You are as drunk as an Indian who doesn't own a business' (this, of course, is based on the observation that serious Indians who run businesses — mostly Muslims — do not drink).

In any society that is strong on stratifying people according to race, those at the bottom layer tend to be vicious with each other.

With the repeal of influx control people from different cultures have suddenly started realising that, after all, they share a common humanity.

There might be slight variations in their cultures, but essentially they all have the same aspirations, share the same ambitions, dreams and so on.

But of course you can't undo long-held prejudices born out of ignorance in just 10 years of freedom.

Because we are still nurturing our new-found sense of common humanity it's only right that we be careful how we tell these jokes, lest we perpetuate racial and ethnic stereotypes.

For example, only when I want the shape of my nose altered can I walk into a pub in Ventersdorp and call the barman a 'boer'; but Afrikaans writer Rian Malan has, in the past, invited me to call him that. I suppose it depends on relationships, familiarity.

Darkies tell interesting jokes among themselves about themselves — but they would get mad if the same jokes were to be told by honkies.

An Afrikaner friend tells me that the acronym AVBOB (the funeral people) stands for, 'Almal Vrek Behalwe Ons Boere' (everyone dies, except for us Afrikaners).

Afrikaners can tell that kind of joke among themselves, but it is frowned upon to have outsiders telling the same joke.

Over the years I've tried to be an equal- opportunity offender, but a Zulu friend wondered why I, a Zulu, was happy to tell abusive jokes about Zulus but was soft on Xhosas.

He forgets that I'm married to a Xhosa. When I started paying ilobolo my in-laws said: 'Mkhwenyana, you're now part of our family.'

Seven years later I am still paying my ilobolo to be part of the superior tribe. Eish!

But then again, exhibiting their admirable intellect, the Xhosas have taught me one good saying which I'm passing on to my children with alacrity: 'Into yomntu ngeyam (What's yours is mine).'

Ja, these Xhosas!

On a more serious note, people of South Africa, it's become fashionable to drag poor Khumalo to the Press Ombudsman for this or that offence. As we speak, I am waiting for him to rule on two cases: one complaint from a Canadian-Swazi, another from a Xhosa.

Take it easy, people. Let's laugh at our idiosyncrasies — with due sensitivity, of course.

8 May 2005

Lack of self-worth makes mockery of Rainbow Nation

FIRST OF ALL, let's dispense with some old chestnuts: we South Africans are a lovely people, a miracle of history, Archbishop Desmond Tutu's rainbow nation.

Not so long ago this country sent former politician and highly respected business-man Cyril Ramaphosa to Ireland where he shared with the warring factions over there South Africa's formula for reconciliation after a long-drawn-out, insidious, albeit muffled racial war of attrition.

Lawyer Fink Haysom has won international kudos for his groundbreaking work in ending tribal friction in Africa's Great Lakes region.

Ah, this feel-good stuff is so powerful we can't help but keep repeating it to ourselves in the hope that it will solve all our other problems.

But the delicious irony of our country is that, in as much as we have taught the world about peaceful coexistence, as individuals making up this nation we are still at odds with our individual self-worth, and therefore the worth of the nation.

Hence the high levels of crime, hence the dysfunctional families, hence the gangrene that's corroding our leaders in both the private and public sectors — unmitigated greed and selfishness that's making a mockery of all the noble intentions of creating equal opportunities for all to gain access to wealth-creation opportunities.

It's as if we don't believe we deserve the international honours that have been bestowed upon us. Indeed, at the rate we are going, we don't deserve the respect the world is giving us. That is the problem: lack of self-worth.

This is a lesson that the Black Consciousness icon Steve Biko tried to inculcate in black people. Stop blaming white people — yes, they are part of the problem as they are propping up the oppressive system under which we find ourselves, but look deeper within yourselves as individual black persons: liberate your minds. Take action to make the necessary amends in your life, in society. Take responsibility.

I think that this, perhaps, also answers the concerns that have been raised by some that Black Consciousness is a negative force as it celebrates race consciousness.

Apartheid created a negative consciousness where people were called non-whites, in which context the centrality of whiteness was overwhelming. If you were to remove the 'white' from non-white you would be left with a 'non', a nothingness.

Now, as we commemorate 30 years since he died, we should remember that Biko never advocated that those who are not black be called non-blacks, exactly because he never exuded a negative energy.

He believed that people should harness their positive energy. In this regard, he was of the opinion that the whites who were sympathetic to the black cause of the time should organise among their own community in support of the black cause. Why?

He was worried that if whites were allowed into the Black Consciousness fold they would inevitably, because of their education and privileged position in society, usurp leadership roles.

Today, we have an open society, with all the trappings of a nascent democracy, thanks to the sacrifices of Biko and others. We are not perfect, but we are getting there.

But the restlessness in the black community is worrisome. Many people who were scarred by a system that told them that they were worthless are still in the grip of this nightmare of inferiority. Many still haven't made peace with who they are, and what they are capable of. That's why the teachings of Black Consciousness will always remain relevant. One is not calling for the formation of a BC organisation; we have plenty of useless organisations as it is. What one is advocating is for those teachings of Biko and the BC movement to be resuscitated and shared in the forums that already exist. His book I Write What I Like should be required reading for all South Africans — so that all sectors of our society can understand each other's points of departure and desired destinations. Biko's are very simple but powerful teachings that have value to all people in this country.

A story in the New York Times recently pointed out that young people who had obese friends or relatives also tended to veer towards obesity. Obesity, as much as it is genetic, has also proved to be a social phenomenon influenced by lifestyle and eating habits.

I would venture to take crime into this mix. I want to hazard an opinion that if you live in a crime- ridden neighbourhood you are bound to regard crime as an inescapable reality of life; as a result you might end up participating, as I have noticed with many people from the township of my childhood. Some of these crimes are committed not out of desperation to make a living, but as a social fad.

There is a lack of a positive consciousness in society.

But more worrisome is that the current dispensation is based on the assumption that all are equal, and that all have equal opportunities; that all should now be able to pull themselves up by their bootstraps. But you can't pull yourself up by the bootstraps if you don't have any boots.

People who are not confident in who they are will have little or no respect for the next human being. And that's exactly what we are seeing now. More than ever before, our communities are plagued by things so alien in their brutality that you wonder where they stem from: the rape of children as young as a few months, the heinous murders, the violent robberies. Because the criminals have no self-respect they have nothing to lose.

I am not talking about crimes committed by the sophisticated layer of society — the corruption in the private sector, the white-collar crime, the almost criminal BEE transactions that make a mockery of empowerment. I am talking about crimes committed by so-called ordinary people.

These are people who hate themselves. For you can't love yourself if you don't know yourself. And if you don't know yourself and don't love yourself, there is no hope in hell that you would have an iota of respect for the next person — regardless of his or her colour, age or station in life.

16 September 2007

There are many rooms in Hostel Blame

MKHIZE AND HIS 10-YEAR-OLD SON were just two hours into their flight from South Africa to London when the plane started to experience engine problems, the story goes. The captain instructed the crew members to jettison the luggage, or the plane would crash.

But even after members of the crew had gotten rid of the last piece of luggage, the plane continued to list and lurch dangerously. Thinking quickly, the captain made a drastic decision and instructed the crew to start getting rid of some of the passengers.

This was to be done alphabetically, according to nationality and/or race. Two Americans on board were thrown out, followed by a couple of Australians. Then it was time to move to the next letter in the alphabet: B.

Mkhize and his son were the only blacks, so they had to go. But Mkhize fought back, denying the obvious fact that he was black. Members of the crew had no time to waste, so they proceeded to get rid of some Caucasians.

Then the plane stabilised. Mkhize's son turned to him: 'But, dad, why did you resist when they tried to get us out of the plane based on our race. Aren't we African after all? Aren't we black?'

'Today, son, we are Zulus. Right at the end of the alphabet,' came the answer.

This morbid joke is usually told by Zulus when they are trying to prove their ability to think on their feet, contrary to the stereotype that Zulus are thick and stubborn — only good enough to fight at taxi ranks and hostels.

It's a story that came to mind this week when my colleague, photographer Simphiwe Nkwali, told me about his trip to Mozambique. He had gone to attend the funeral of Ernesto Alfabeto Nhamuave, the man who was burned alive during the attacks on foreigners in the Ramaphosa informal settlement on the East Rand.

Nkwali told of the anger of the Mozambican people against Zulus, who have been reported as being central to the xenophobic attacks.

Nkwali had to lie about his heritage in the face of the naked anger; he had to deny his association with Zulus. Ironically, Nkwali, who had taken the picture of the burning man, had been the first photographer to track down the family of this stranger because he wanted to be sure the body received a proper burial. Nkwali also helped to transport the charred remains of the Mozambican back to his native land.

Still, his affinity with Zulus had rendered him persona non grata in Mozambique.

This is sad. Sad because the allegation that Zulus are central to the attacks is not backed up by logic or concrete facts.

Let's start with the allegation that the xenophobic South Africans, on encountering a 'suspicious-looking' person, will ask him the Zulu word for elbow to ascertain that he is South African. It's a story that has been repeated so many times it has become 'the truth'.

In fact, it's an urban legend that dates back to the politically inspired violence that befell in what is now known as KwaZulu-Natal in the late '80s and early '90s, when Zulu attackers were rumoured to be using the same trick to weed out Xhosas in their midst who did not know that the Zulu word for elbow is indololwane and not ingqiniba, as in Xhosa.

It is against this background that I have serious doubts about the veracity of the indololwane story, or that Zulus are central to the attacks.

So, too, it's instructive that the number of xenophobic attacks in KwaZulu-Natal have been minimal.

Also, I cannot understand why xenophobic tormentors would use one's ability to speak Zulu as a measure of one's South African-ness. When foreigners arrive in this country, the first local language they are most likely to learn is Zulu — it's a dominant language, and it's simple.

Another factor to consider: the Zimbabweans from Bulawayo and other Ndebele-speaking parts of that country are more Zulu than, say, Venda-speaking South Africans. The Ndebele left South Africa during King Shaka's time, but the language they speak and the customs and traditions they hold dear have their roots in the Zulu culture. It is therefore preposterous that the xenophobic tormentors would use the Zulu language in order to weed out the so-called foreigners.

Xenophobic tormentors really intent on weeding out 'foreigners' would use a more complex language — Pedi or Venda, for example.

When those Vendas start talking, it's like they are singing, or reciting a profound poem. Very few South Africans understand the language. Better still, if the xenophobes did not want to use Venda or Pedi, they would subject their quarry to the challenging clicks of Xhosa: iqaqa laziqikaqika eqawukeni kaqhawuka uqhoqhoqho!!

I would therefore take the indololwane story for what it is — a destructive, divisive urban legend meant to set Zulu-speaking South Africans against people from the Southern African region. It's simply illogical.

It's unfortunate that, while we managed to be a united front against apartheid, the issue of tribe or race keeps rearing its ugly head with alarming frequency these days — especially when there's conflict.

These references to race and ethnic origin tell me a bitter truth: once the foreigners are no longer a problem, we will be left all by ourselves in this sad game of blaming the next person for our unfortunate circumstances.

That's not a pleasant thought.

For now, please leave us Zulus alone so we can concentrate on the things we do best: taking care of our taxis and hostels.

8 June 2008

How many Zulus does it take to change a light bulb?

NAME-DROPPING IS A JOURNALIST'S INEVITABLE PASTIME. You can have a whisky with the president in the afternoon, talk about BEE deals with the likes of Cyril Ramaphosa, one of the country's new generation of top-flight businessmen, in the evening, have social intercourse with prostitutes at night — all in the line of duty, of course.

The reason I am starting this column with this disclaimer is that I am about to do a very bizarre kind of name-dropping.

Here goes: Sibusiso Zuma, the Bafana Bafana star, is not only black like me, he is also Zulu like me. And not only that, he also comes from my township of Mpumalanga, Hammarsdale. Furthermore, he used to play for the same amateur soccer side as my younger brother, Thabo.

But now we have a problem, me and my homeboy, Sibusiso. After years of playing soccer overseas he was back in the country recently at the invitation of a sports goods company.

A friend tells me that Zuma was surprised to find himself the centre of attention. I wondered why he was surprised, until he explained that it wasn't his soccer prowess that had attracted the attention but the fact that everyone was calling him Msholozi.

To Zulu people, Msholozi is a common clan name for those with the surname Zuma. But to non-Zulus, Msholozi conjures up the face of Jacob Zuma, hence Sibusiso Zuma's concern that he is being associated with all the bad tales being told about the former deputy president.

I can appreciate his discomfort. I've been down that road, where you hear people sniggering about Zulus and showers.

Not so long ago, the sectors of South African society that were at the receiving end of bad jokes were the Shangaans and the Van der Merwes.

But the shower-and-baby-oil combo has given them some breathing space — at the expense of the noble savages of KwaZulu-Natal.

The other day I held the floor telling a story about why Shangaan men have big penises. When a Shangaan boy is born, his father plants a tree. As the tree grows, so does the manhood. When the father thinks the tree has grown to an acceptable size, he cuts down the tree. Correspondingly, the penis stops growing.

I wondered aloud, what if, while the penis-tree is still growing in the Shangaan family garden, a flood hits the township, washes the tree away, down to the seashore, where it takes root and continues to grow and grow, reaching for the heavens.

Imagine the boy running around in a panic, shouting: 'Where is my penis-tree? My father needs to cut it down now!'

In the past, I have tested this story on many discerning jokers, and they have given it the thumbs up, especially the Shangaan jokers. But this time around, my audience just looked at me blankly, and a Swazi guy shook his head and said: 'Khumalo, your tongue is dirty. It needs a Zulu shower.'

I had never seen a Swazi guy being so gallant against a Zulu. After all, when we attacked the Swazis aeons ago, their brave response was to run to the mountaintop. Once there, they showered us with insults.

Later, when their king asked them how they had dealt with the Zulus, they said: 'Ngwe-nyama, mlomo longacali manga, sibatfukile!' meaning, 'Oh, king, The Mouth Which Doesn't Tell Lies, we just showered them with such heavy insults they had no option but to run away.'

But this time around, the Swazi guy's retort against me and my dirty mouth drew howls of laughter. Then more Zulu jokes were thrown at me with amazing intensity.

A Tswana guy told one about how the Aids virus is going around with bagfuls of money. Every time the virus meets a potential victim it shows him or her wads of money and says: 'Are you Zulu?'

If the person responds in the affirmative, the virus smiles broadly and says: 'I would like to be friends with you. In fact, I want to give you all this money ...'

'What's the catch?' the Zulu asks.

'Promise me you will never take a shower again!'

I was in Port Elizabeth for the launch of my book the other day and, instead of staying at the hotel, I slept at a friend's place. Before we said our goodnights, she asked: 'Are you going to shower now or in the morning?'

I almost jumped in alarm at the mention of that word 'shower'. Why does she think I need to shower now? What does she think I've been up to? Is she saying this to me just because I'm Zulu?

It is against this background that I think I understand and appreciate Sibusiso Zuma's discomfort with his Zuluness.

When David Medalie launched his novel "The Shadow Follows", recently, he encouraged South Africans to laugh at themselves.

You satirise something because you hope that, by doing so, you can bring about change, he said. I wonder what these Zulu jokes are going to change about the character of the Zulu person.

Now, whenever I move in public places, I seem to notice Zulus clustered together, talking quietly, or sullenly looking deep into their glasses, sighing, perhaps wondering when these Zulu jokes are going to come to an end, so attention can happily refocus on the Shangaans and the Van der Merwes.

4 June 2006

Writers in search of a new country

IT WAS ONE OF THOSE DELICIOUSLY IRONIC MOMENTS: a newspaper journalist being interviewed by a Nobel laureate for literature.

VS Naipaul had quietly sneaked into South Africa, and set about interviewing a cross-section of locals for his next book, an ambitious tome focusing on African religions and African spirituality.

While Sir Vidia, the appropriate address since his knighthood, has written numerous texts about the continent, both fictional and non-fictional, his search for new material has taken him to Nigeria, Uganda and Gabon.

Friends vehemently tried to dissuade him and his wife, Nadira, herself a writer, from coming to South Africa ('Are you mad? Do you have death wishes? That is the crime capital of the world.').

Sir Vidia, who was once described by a critic as an eagle who sits high on his perch and watches everything below — and misses nothing, decided he wanted to come to South Africa for this book, which, he says, will be his last in a career spanning more than five decades.

They say water flows because of gravity; people flow because of symbols. And on the continent, attractive symbols lie in the south. South Africa epitomises the continent in all its complexity: a wounded history, multiculturalism, the restlessness and, most importantly, hope.

It was therefore inevitable that Sir Vidia would succumb to gravity and venture south.

He had read about the racial problems of our country's past but what struck him upon his arrival was more than the residue of the past. He had not expected such a multiplicity of identities — which extend beyond black and white. There are cultural identities (I am Zulu before I am South African), religious identities (I am Muslim before I am South African), sexual identities (I am gay before I am South African) and many others.

And overshadowing all of these identities is the obsession with race.

Sir Vidia set about identifying his targets, people he would speak to in an attempt to unravel the cultural/religious story of post-apartheid South Africa. At some stage he spoke to a kwaito artist, who told him Nelson Mandela had betrayed black people. He compromised too much.

In addition to the controversial kwaito artist, Sir Vidia decided to interview a journalist. Ignoring protestations from the journalist that journos are not good interviewing material, the world-renowned author and thinker insisted on meeting the journalist at his own house — 'because he can only make a judgement on the character he is interviewing once he has seen him [the character] in his own environment', his aide explained.

It's always touching and amazing to look at one's country through other people's eyes. They see what your eyes skip past or what you subconsciously choose to ignore. Issues such as the race question.

The interaction between Sir Vidia, his wife and the journalist spread over three nights, during which they spoke over tea, enjoyed dinner and went to the theatre to see a play that draws upon our immediate past in order to better understand the present.

Sir Vidia wanted to know: why the obsession with race when Mandela had already set the tone for a non-racial dispensation?

When a South African speaks about a fellow countryman he is bound to say something like: 'I am talking about that Indian guy with a big beard', and so on.

Sir Vidia could not help remarking on how race is used descriptively. The journalist responded that 15 years is too soon for us to shake off the yoke of race.

We come from a past where a white person with only a Std 4 education was deemed superior to Dr Nthato Motlana or Dr AB Xuma, with all their education and international exposure — by virtue of the colour of his skin.*

We come from a past where black people could not own houses in the cities and suburbs, even if they could afford them. That's the racial crucible in which we were shaped.

Mandela and Tutu's exhortation to the nation to embrace non-racialism after 1994 provided warm and positive symbolism that the nation needed at that time, a crutch it could use to hobble into a new country in pursuit of a rather elusive non-racial consciousness.

At this point in the discussion Nadira noted that some of her friends blamed the resurgence of race-consciousness on Thabo Mbeki.

However, she disagreed. She thought Mbeki was correct when he made his observation about South Africa being a country of two nations — one rich and white, and the other black and poor. He had to make the country pause to take stock before blindly singing an empty non-racial song, she argued.

The journalist pointed out that Mbeki-bashing had become a national pastime. Nowadays everyone hates Mbeki and what he stood for, even in instances when he was correct.

Those who supported Mbeki during his tenure have become as scarce as hen's teeth or, more appropriately, as scarce as the white people who propped up apartheid for more than four decades.

When Mbeki made his two-nations remark he was only, like a journalist, reporting on what he was seeing on the ground. That there were a few black billionaires who had sprouted overnight did not erase the reality of millions of poorly educated, unemployed and starving black people next to millions of whites with a good education, secure jobs and roofs over their heads.

The journalist continued: 'Personally, I am an optimist and in the left wing and sometimes liberal circles that I move in, even though we are conscious of race we choose not to obsess over it. When we comfort ourselves as South Africans we always pat each other on the back, and say: 'Ah, thank God the past is over. We have moved on.'

"Moved on to what exactly?", Sir Vidia wanted to know.

The journalist hesitated before responding that the country had jettisoned statutory racism — and was now in a limbo, caught between that terrible past and the uncertain future. The legacy of the past is too great to shake off easily as the nation trudges, uncertainly, towards the utopia of non-racialism.

"There is a danger, though", intervened Sir Vidia, "that the obsession with race might prove counter-productive in the long run". He referred to the experience of his native Trinidad. For a long time that country hobbled along as a nation of Indo-Trinidadians and Afro-Trinidadians, and some other minorities. There was tension (subtle as it was at times) between the races.

Sir Vidia noted, sadly, that during the tenure of Eric Williams, a one-time black-power adherent who reigned as prime minister from 1956 until his death in 1981, the island was in the grip of a sad form of race consciousness.

While it might have been an attempt to empower the descendants of slaves, the race consciousness tended to racialise everything, with debilitating results, he argued.

But over the years the tensions ebbed and the country embraced a state of nation-hood where individuals saw themselves as Trinidadians. Period. No ethnic prefixes.

"How did the Trinidadians do it", the journalist wondered.

"Time healed the wounds", Sir Vidia responded. "But, he added, the people also spoke about the problem rather than sweeping it under the carpet".

On that note, both Sir Vidia and the journalist, moi, agreed.

If South Africans don't continue to speak openly about the problem, we will remain a 'simple' people, said Sir Vidia. By 'simple' people he meant those who lack intellectual rigour, who lack a moral backbone, who lack a vision of who they would like to be as a nation; a people who, when they lose an argument, resort to race.

Again, the journalist agreed.

*Motlana and Xuma were prominent medical doctors with a high political profile not only in the black community but in the entire nation. Xuma became president of the ANC, while Motlana, after quitting medicine, became one of the forerunners of black economic empowerment.

Oh baby, it's a white world …

First it was Jacob Zuma with his Umshini Wam song; then President "Thibo Touch" Mabeki – that's the nickname of former president Thabo Mbeki - came to the fore with his intention to record a song in an attempt to woo the kwaito generation to the ranks of his support base.

Everyone seems to be waking up to the power of music as a strategy to win the hearts and minds of society, whose attention span is fast becoming that of a fruit fly.

Being a student of Mzwakhe Mbuli's school of poetry, I thought it was time I put my talents to good use.

The poem I've written, I think, will work wonders if sung to the melody of James Brown's 'This is a Man's World'.

Aptly entitled 'This is a White, White, White World', the poem is intended as a balm to heal the racial angst that is eating away at our society — from Parliament, where DA and ANC MPs are exchanging racial insults, down to the courts, where the judiciary is riven by racial prejudice; from strip joints, where a guy called Lolly is spewing racial venom; to private homes, where people who slaughter their beasts are accused of being barbaric.

    So here goes:

This is a white world, this is a white, white world
But it would be nothing
Nothing without a darkie to care.
You see, whitey made the cars
To take us over the road
Whitey made white man's liquor
To help darkie carry the heavy load
Whitey takes darkie to school
Whitey makes darkie a judge in a court of law
And darkie drinks too much white man's liquor
Drives white man's car into a white man's wall
And that ain't cool,
Ain't cool at all
In this white, white world.
Whitey tells Michael Jackson, your nose is ugly
And Wacko Jacko then gets a nose job and a chin to match.
Jackson gets a whitey complexion
And thinks he is a whitey.
Wacko Jacko looks real wacko with a face falling apart,
Well, dear, serves you right!
And so a little black darkie, Obama
Whose name sounds just like Osama,
Wants to be the US makhulu baas
But whitey won't have no darkie baas
Get back to your barracks, Obama
Now's not your time, Obama,
Not when we still haven't found Osama.
In this white, white world.
Whitey made the Gautrain to carry the heavy load
But darkie blocked the Gautrain in its tracks.

Is it alright, is it alright, is it alright if I screeeaaam?
Yeaaah!
Whitey made the electro lights
To take us out of the dark,
But Eskom said get back into the dark, you darkies.
Is it alright, is it alright, is it alright if I screaaam?
Yeeeah!
Darkie tries to slaughter his own bull,
With his own spear,
In his own back yard.
Whitey says, oh dear,
You sure are backward
Don't you know it's bloody cruel.
Darkie says let's get affirmative action
So we can level the playing fields
But whitey says, no reverse discrimination,
That's a real abomination
In this white, white world.
Whitey made the bullet for the war
But darkie went for the arms deal for sure
And a lot of money was made for sure,
While some short-sighted darkies only got discounted 4x4s.
This is a white, white world,
But it would be nothing
Nothing without a darkie to scare.
Whitey thinks of our little baby girls
And the baby boys
Whitey makes them happy, 'cause whitey makes them toys
And whitey takes them to Teazers and the Grand
And Lolly Jackson overcharges the darkie children
Says it's not in their culture to play at strip joints;
Says a darkie child has a girlfriend here and there,

Darkie child has one girlfriend in this homeland
And in the next shackland,
Darkie child has got even another girl he's gonna have a shower with tomorrow
Not a nice innuendo, this thing about a shower tomorrow ...
But what can we say,
This is a white, white world.
President says, Crime ain't no crisis,
In this country of darkies owned by whiteys,
There's no crisis, no crime crisis at all.
Crime will only be out of control
When darkies say it is.
Is it alright, is it alright, is it alright if I screaaaam?
Yeaaaaah!

19 July 2009

Of Politics And Politicians

The boy in the bubble

WHERE I COME FROM we have a nice little word that can be used to describe Julius Malema: ihlongandlebe. There is no English equivalent for this Zulu word but many choose to translate it as 'a contumelious nincompoop'.

I think they are giving him undue credit when they call him a rude fool. Whereas a rude fool is very much in charge of his faculties — knowing when to reach full tilt in his rudeness, and when to step back and gather steam so he can pounce again — the 27-year-old Malema knows no such subtleties.

He reacts to controversy like a shark drawn to blood — and like a shark, he can only move forward.

So I choose to regard him as my own version of ihlongandlebe, where the word means a person who was dropped on his head when he was a baby.

We all know what those who were dropped on their heads when they were babies behave like or think like, when they get thinking at all.

Malema's history — if the word 'history' can be debased so as to describe the incoherent string of incidents that are the total sum of the boy's life — is littered with insinuations of one not very in charge of his intellectual and verbal faculties.

This intellectual invalid repeated both grades 8 and 9. And even after spending seven years at secondary school, he did not even achieve a matric exemption.

Commenting on why he failed two consecutive grades Malema did not shrink in embarrassment, but gladly stated that he failed because he could not contain his excitement about joining Cosas (Congress of South African Students).

Another misnomer: the word 'student' should refer to one who studies. But our boy with very little in his head does not seem to have spent any length of time studying anything, except stuffing his damaged head with all manner of trite sloganeering.

'I got excited after joining Cosas and failed grade 8. In 1997, I was expelled for political activities and pleaded to be taken back, and I repeated grade 9 in 1998.'

There was a time in our history when it was de rigueur to write in one's CV: 'Qualifications: BA (University of Fort Hare) — studies incomplete due to political involvement.'

I know many ministers who have that in their CVs. It's understandable. They were uprooted from their classes by the apartheid police, many of them ending up in jail, others in exile.

But common sense tells me that if I were in the shoes of someone who was expelled from school three years into our democracy, I wouldn't take pride in that.

But hell, who is accusing Malema of having an iota of common sense?

About his academic peregrinations (or lack thereof?) Malema also once bared his heart to a reporter: '[While at school] I was a gentleman and used to wear a school uniform. I was not always in school because of organisational activities. Last year [2001] I moved to Joburg and an arrangement was made by the two departments (Gauteng and Limpopo education departments). I attended classes at Prudence Secondary School and wrote my exams at Mohlakeng.'

Themba Sepotokele, who wrote the story, added this caveat: 'Attempts to confirm there had been such an arrangement were unsuccessful.'

Nice touch, Mr Reporter.

Malema was, at the time of the interview, under the spotlight for leading a rampage through the streets of Johannesburg by thousands of unruly pupils who looted, stole and smashed car windows as they went — ostensibly to protest against a Gauteng Department of Education directive that schools close their gates during teaching hours for safety reasons.

Malema seems to have something against issues relating to safety.

He allegedly organised members of the ANCYL to disrupt the funeral of the late Norman Mashabane to prevent his arch enemy, Limpopo premier Sello Moloto, from addressing the mourners.

This led to some ANCYL members being beaten and thrown out of the stadium.

The same pattern was followed at the national congress where Malema was made president of the ANCYL: fisticuffs were exchanged and his supporters exposed their buttocks to challengers to the throne.

Again, Malema did not find anything insane about this behaviour. In fact, when he threw a farewell party for his predecessor, Fikile Mbalula, the other day he told him that 'there is a new president' at the ANCYL and Mbalula was no longer to hang around.

'I know that there are these presidents who have a tendency not to like handing over (a snide reference to President Mbeki). If the youth does something wrong they come and say this is not how we do things in our youth league. This is not your youth league, Mbalula, you led a different youth league. You did not have to deal with naked people at your congress. Our youth league congress had naked people all over the place, yours didn't!'

So, I wasn't very surprised when he said he and his comrades were prepared to kill in defence of Zuma.

People look at him, an elected leader of the ANCYL and thus a potential future leader of this country, and quickly conclude that the boy-who-was-dropped-on-his-head is a reflection of the best brains and talent this country has to offer.

After all, the youth league produced the likes of Advocate Anton Lembede, Nelson Mandela and others, and it is therefore logical to expect the next cadre of leaders to come from this body.

But the aforementioned gentlemen did not shy away from school, believing that isikolo sinendawo yaso (school has its own role), as the Xhosas say.

Now, there's food for thought for those who were not dropped on their heads when they were young.

On second thoughts, I think I have to thank the gods of academia for denying Malema the stamina for rigorous study.

Imagine a highly educated Malema. He would be going all over the place like one Ronald Suresh Roberts, insulting everyone who disagrees with his notion of what makes a good intellectual, or a good analyst, or a good politician, or a good human being, for that matter. Now, there's a real ihlongandlebe.

Malema's problem does not end with his education; it's got everything to do with his head. But let me stop there before I get sued.

22 June 2008

Zoom, Zoom, Zoom, Zumatime!

WITHOUT ANY SINGING OF IT, as Alan Paton would have said, South Africa is one of the most beautiful countries in the world — the people, the weather, the scenery and, of course, the politics.

Especially the politics.

The splendour of the country is much in evidence during the month of December, when people, most of whom don't have to wake up early and head off to work, are in a jovial and relaxed mood.

Those of us who have families spread all over the country are lucky in that we get to visit our relatives during this month and are, in the process, showered with the richness of this country.

I was lucky to spend Christmas day in three different cities, thanks to that invention by the Wright brothers, the airplane. I had my breakfast in Johannesburg, enjoyed my first piece of braaied meat of the festive season with my parents in Durban and had oodles more meat later that day with my in-laws in Cape Town, where two sheep had been slaughtered for a traditional ceremony.

Apart from the beauty of the people and the traditional beer that followed me from Durban to the Cape, this loveliness expressed itself in their sense of humour and tenacious engagement with the future of the country.

No sooner had I told my parents that I wouldn't be spending the rest of Christmas day with them than a whole troop of neighbours was summoned to our yard to welcome the Son From Johannesburg, yes, he of the arrogant newspapers, to answer a few questions about where the country was going.

Now, I am not a sangoma, and I work for a newspaper that has the audacity to show The Leader with a shower head,* but they come to me for answers about the state of the nation. I danced around the question, and instead started a traditional song. The group soon picked it up, we started singing rowdily. But no singing is complete in KwaZulu-Natal without someone invoking the machine gun. Inevitably, when the singing stopped, and we sat around the fire and turned those steaks around to brown properly, someone had to revive the topic: 'Real men don't eat meat that's overcooked; ask real men like Zuma.' Sigh.

'When Zuma wins those court cases against you disrespectful newspaper people, we will celebrate and have loads of meat,' someone said. Sigh!

I grew up in a culture where meat, traditional beer, women, soccer and a bit of fighting were favourite topics among our menfolk. Now, Zuma has taken precedence over all of that. Amazing stuff.

So, off I jetted to Cape Town, where I thought I would experience some respite from politics. It was not to be. Even in Cape Town, as we sat around eating meat and talking about issues of nationhood, ranging from why our men were shirking their responsibilities as heads of their families to why our children were obsessed with TV at the expense of books, the topic magically veered off to Zuma. Is he going to be our president; if not, why not? What can we expect of his leadership?

When someone pointed out that our president was, in fact, Kgalema Motlanthe** there was a momentary silence, all eyes turned to the speaker, and the stares seemed to suggest that he was demented. Even though I wanted to echo the speaker's sentiments I decided to shut up and allow the discussion — such as it was — to follow its natural course. And the tenor of the discussion was how the powers-that-be were out to get Zuma.

The Congress of the People, that opportunistic break-away party from the ruling ANC, they said, was a creation by the West to distract The People from their project of bringing true liberation to The Masses. There were conspiracy theories galore, so much so that I thought to myself: Aha, Mugabe is a good teacher in the school of what Albert Camus would have called The Absurd.

Tomorrow I fly to France, where I will be lecturing and writing for a month and a bit at an artistic institution. As I pack, my heart is suffused with the hope that this year will be politically saner than the year that was dominated by The-One-Who-Was-Dropped-On-His-Head-When-He-Was-Young. Let's think with our heads, not with our hearts.

For what it's worth, let's take a leaf from Zuma's book — sing and dance through our difficulties and challenges. After all, Zuma takes his lead from none other than Nietzsche, who exhorted his fellow existentialists: 'Il faut danser la vie (life should be danced)'. Without any singing of it, this country is wonderful, and this year let's build on that beauty.

*Ah, in case you've forgotten, cartoonist Zapiro (real name Jonathan Shapiro) added a shower head to his caricatures of Zuma after the man, appearing in court in 2006 accused of having raped a woman who was HIV positive, told the court that after having sex with the woman, he took a shower. The nation was left to conclude that he considered taking a shower a precaution against the virus. Zapiro used the shower head device to highlight what he perceived as the president's irresponsible behaviour, and the ill-thought-out message he was sending to the nation.

** Motlanthe was interim president after the unceremonious firing of President Mbeki. He is remembered as the cool-headed man who warmed the seat of power for Zuma.

4 June 2009

Revolutionary tongues: the Zulus and the French

IF THERE IS ANY COMMONALITY between the South African masses, especially the Zulus, and their French counterparts, it is simply that they love a good fight.

The French routed the ruling classes and gave the world their revolution in 1789, and we South Africans humiliated the Brits and gave the world the battle of Isandlwana in 1879.

The French gave the world the guillotine, and we delivered the necklace.

Okay, now, let's not get carried away — those were extremes. But you get the drift; both our nations are fighters.

In South Africa we get whipped into a frenzy of toyi-toying at the slightest provocation. Somebody proposes a name change for some obscure street in Bapetikosweti, and we toyi-toyi either for or against it.

Peter Marais crosses the floor and we toyi-toyi — even before we know which party this serial floor-crosser is going to join this time.

I've been here in France for just over a month and have lost count of the strikes they've had. Every other day there is a strike at the harbour across the road from where I'm staying.

I think the French, if they had their way, would toyi-toyi in front of God's gate against the terrible weather.

They love striking.

Nationally, there has been quite a serious strike to protest against the right-wing government of Nicolas Sarkozy and how it has handled the economy.

I felt a glow of joy when I saw them burning tyres in the streets. It felt like home. I wanted to join them.

But I couldn't. My hands were full: a baguette in one hand and a glass of Bordeaux red in the other.

I was taught as a kid that it is bad table manners to dance while you are eating. So all I could do, between mouthfuls, was to shout encouragement: 'Vive la revolution, comrades!'

Anyway, to get to the serious part of this: I went to address a group of students at the University of Nantes the other day. It made me proud that they were doing a degree course in what they call South African civilisation, which covers our politics, literature, film and so forth.

How humbling.

One of the movies they had seen as part of the course was Hijack Stories, and they kept asking me if this gritty movie was based on the truth.

I wished I could tell them it wasn't.

Anyway, my address almost didn't take place as there was — you've guessed it — a strike at the university. A serious one.

It involved both teachers and students and related to the government's funding of education.

The government wanted to shirk its responsibility to fund the universities, according to the people who tried to simplify the complicated picture for me.

But the government was not being forthright and telling the institutions and their people what its intentions are.

No, the government, like all good governments in the good civilised world that gave us the credit crunch, was using polite-speak, spin-speak, to say: 'No, we are not cutting funds, we are merely giving you universities autonomy'.

Autonomy, my foot.

Thankfully, a lot of these people – students and teachers alike – were not dumb.

Rumour had it that the strategy was to privatise, for lack of a better word, the universities. You appoint somebody who is good at keeping a balance sheet. It doesn't matter if he is the former CEO of a rivet-making company, as long as he is good with figures — no pedagogical inclinations necessary. Just run the blerrie university as a business operation.

In France, tertiary education had been very cheap, almost free, thus far.

With the new Sarkozy plan, this might change, and everyone was fighting.

'Even those right-wing people at Paris universities have joined the strike,' one of my informants told me, expressing incredulity at the power of the strike.

How I wished we could have fought the same fight to keep university education affordable in South Africa.

Maybe it's too late now. But, hey, the revolution does not have a sell-by date.

Having addressed my group of students I was on the train back to my apartment when I had a light-bulb moment. Einstein, here I am.

Seeing that I had thus far failed to impress the French — I can't speak their language,

Revolutionary tongues: the Zulus and the French

I can't withstand their cold weather — I thought I should come up with something to bowl them over, seeing as I was about to leave their shores.

I thought that at the next demonstration or strike I should teach them and lead them in the singing of Umshini Wam, Jacob Zuma's favourite liberation song, so they could see my revolutionary credentials.

And not only would I sing Umshini Wam, for crying out loud, I would translate the blerrie thing into French and teach them the melody!

As soon as I arrived at the apartment, I got my pen and paper ready, hauled out my English-French dictionary and started humming in Zulu.

I wondered, for the first time, how Steve Hofmeyr would sing Umshini in Afrikaans. Ah, the United Nations in song!

So I started writing the new, fresh-as-French-polony version: 'Ma mitraillete, ma mitraillete; passé-moi ma mitraillete; ma mitraillete ...'

It looked good on paper, Grammy-award-winning stuff, I thought. Until I opened my mouth to sing it.

The French 'r' is pretty harsh on that funny pink lump of meat at the back of my throat. Every time I say my name in full in the French manner, I feel sore in the throat.

So, by the time I had practised my French Umshini Wam a few times, I realised how raw my throat felt.

A glass of Bordeaux red was in order. And some rest.

The revolution could wait. It has no sell-by date.

22 February 2009

The King and I

LESSON NUMBER ONE: don't mess with the king of the Zulus if you are a South African who aspires to some power and influence in business and in society.

Many businessmen trying to penetrate the black market but who forgot to treat the king with due courtesy and respect have, over the years, burnt their fingers.

Remember when the lottery authorities launched their marketing campaign under the slogan 'Tata machance, tata mamillions'?

The king and his subjects objected loudly to grammatical errors in what was sold as a Zulu slogan. The correct slogan should have been thatha ama-chance (which, in itself, is not pure Zulu).

Anyway, the lotto administrators had to quietly resort to a new jingle.

Now the book I've just finished reading: Black Jerusalem, by advertising guru Happy Ntshingila, further amplifies the influence of the king over these matters of public discourse.

The author learned the lesson first hand when he was head of the first black-owned and black-run ad agency, Herdbuoys.

Ntshingila and his two partners, the suave Peter Vundla and the ebullient Dimape Serenyane, thought they were on top of their game, clevahs from Soweto who had intimate knowledge and understanding of the black market.

Turns out that they were in fact kalakoens (township argot for dumb asses), who had forgotten to pay due attention to one crucial component of the black market — the touchy Zulus, who are particular about their language and their king.

One of Herdbuoys' clients was, at that time, South African Breweries (SAB), who were having problems with Castle Milk Stout, for a long time a black brand. The political climate, which started changing in the early 1990s, brought with it new developments in the economic sector as well. Black people were gradually moving up the economic ladder, in the process abandoning what had hitherto been considered their 'traditional' fare.Milk Stout was one of these, and it was huge in KwaZulu-Natal.

With some nimble footwork Herdbuoys produced a series of memorable ads that immediately turned the fortunes of the ailing stout.

But one of these adverts did not go down well with King Goodwill. And when you mess with the king you can't predict what his subjects will do to you. Do you ever mess with the taxi men?

Ntshingila writes in his book about this particular ad, which got my people's goat: 'The storyline concerned the various "pitches" made to a traditional chief by three suitors, each requesting his daughter's hand in marriage. The first two extolled their virtues, which were riches and physical strength respectively, to an unimpressed daughter. But the third talked of purity of heart and nobility of spirit, which really did it for this girl.'

Alas, the poor suitor used 'Bayede' in addressing the father. Big oops. Only a reigning Zulu monarch can be addressed as Bayede.

But the Herdbuoys didn't know this. It didn't help that the ad had been written by a Zulu guy, Sandile Mkhasibe. Methinks he had hung out too much with the big kalakoens from Soweto — Ntshingila, Vundla and Serenyane — and had forgotten his roots.

For his sins, Herdbuoys chief kalakoen, Ntshingila, was summoned to a meeting with the king at which he, and chief kalakoen at the SAB, Tony van Kralingen, were given a tongue lashing. But the gracious king extended his royal hand in friendship at the end of the meeting.

The moral of the story is that, as South Africans, we need to respect each other's cultural proclivities, but the manner in which kalakoen Ntshingila tells his story is so humorous you lose sight of the fact that he is still apologising to the king, and preaching to would-be sinners to be careful when dealing with Zulu royalty.

The book is a rip-roaring tour de force that takes you into the heart of the advertising industry — the politics, the backstabbing, the ego-tripping and the downright stupidity of some of the so-called captains of industry.

With Herdbuoys cornering the black market, the market of the future, the big white boys in the industry were getting worried. It came to pass, then, that one of the biggies, McCann-Erickson, an international conglomerate, went into partnership with Herdbuoys.

Although they retained a controlling stake in the new agency, Herdbuoys was never to be the same again. First, the culture shock: staffers from the old McCann-Erickson — white and not used to working with black people — complained that they couldn't do a stitch of work as the black colleagues were noisy. Black management responded by saying, no, they were not noisy; they were simply happy.

I can relate to this. Where I work there is a sports reporter who shall remain nameless about whom many complaints have been whispered by white colleagues — except that they can't confront him, he is so quick with his tongue; and black people complain that white people turn the aircon to freezing levels; maybe it's got to do with their European genes — they enjoy the cold?

Anyway, at the new big agency tensions were bad enough at junior level, but at senior level they were even worse. There's a passage in the book describing how some big shot at McCann's offices in London felt that the guys in South Africa were mishandling one of their major clients, Coca-Cola. So the big shot, Ben Langdon was his name, sent an email to Ntshingila, exhorting him to sort out the mess. To which Ntshingila responded: 'Dear Ben, Piss off'. Talk about chutzpah.

It's lovely to live in a multicultural setting where everyone has a take on the next person — and assumes that the person's behaviour is influenced by his racial background.

When I was still a journalism student I couldn't help noticing that whenever I asked a touchy question in class some lecturers thought I was 'cheeky', but if the same question came from a white classmate, he was considered 'analytical and critical'. (Ah, there he goes again, whipping off the race card, Khumalo with a chip on the shoulder.) Well, for your information, in these trying economic times I can't afford to put chips on my shoulder; I eat them!

This is an important book, as it shows the underbelly of the advertising industry, but it also puts a microscope to the skein of humanity we call the nation of South Africa.

With the Herdbuoys' success there was a sudden mushrooming of other black ad agencies. It's always good to have a role model to look up to. But one of the new guys on the block was an agency called Azaguys, which, right from the onset, did not endear itself to the Soweto kalakoens.

Ntshingila writes about Azaguys: 'What made matters even more interesting was the chief Azaguy himself, Sipho Luthuli ... who was to advertising what Mike Tyson is to the evolution of man.' Ouch!

What I know, having done a stint at an ad agency myself, is that you have to have a thick skin as an adman, an ability to fight, cajole and, sometimes, even grovel.

One of the most colourful clients kalakoen Ntshingila tells us about is well known in business and political circles. The said respectable personage was a makhulubaas at South African Tourism when Herdbuoys pitched for this account.

They put a lot of work into the presentation, and put it on powerpoint, which was still a new discovery in this country. Somewhere in the middle of the presentation, the makhulubaas started snoring. As they were winding up the presentation, the makhulubaas woke up and said: 'Where's the creatives?' Teeheehee.

Ntshingila and his colleagues were justifiably pissed off.

Ntshingila writes: 'We did, however, learn two things from this exercise. Number 1: (the snoring executive) The then chairman of Nail Outdoor, Lliso Consulting, Hertz Car Hire, Business Trust, ANC National Elections Committee, Parliamentary Committee on Committees, deputy chairman of Standard Bank, director of VW, Murray & Roberts, Liberty Group and ex-CEO at Transnet and SA Tourism is a tired, tired man. Number 2: Powerpoint is indeed the soporific everyone claims it to be.'

The snoring exec was Saki Macozoma, ANC bigwig and top-notch businessman.

7 June 2009

Tibo's monkey

TIBO WAS A CHILDHOOD ACQUAINTANCE OF MINE who was famous for some peculiarly baffling reasons. In fact, his name was not even Tibo (his 'school name' was Paulos) — it's just that he owned a rickety bicycle which boasted a rubber horn that made the noise 'tibo-tibo-tibo' when he squeezed it.

Apart from his bicycle, Tibo was also famous in our Unit 3 section of Hammarsdale township, KwaZulu-Natal, for his unusually thick lips. Some children would go 'tibo-tibo-tibo' while pulling their lips in a grotesque and mocking manner when he was passing by.

But Tibo was most famous for the fact that his uncle owned a monkey, a pet that was generally frowned upon by adults, who associated it with witchcraft and all the other nonsense with which older people tried to poison our minds.

We children loved Tibo's uncle's monkey. It roamed their yard freely, but when it got too naughty they put it on a leash — a long chain which was in turn tied to a tall pole. At the pinnacle of the pole was a nice, tiny box or enclosure where the monkey slept or sat and ate snacks when it was not playing with us.

The monkey was fun to us because it was always happy, always willing to co-operate and carry out orders. You could teach it to dance to music, or perform what looked like karate moves, and then you would reward it with a banana or a handful of peanuts, or whatever was available. But some of us gave it stones covered in shiny chocolate-eclair wrappers. You could see its face falling in disappointment upon making the nasty discovery, ag shame!

Tibo's uncle decided to retaliate by teaching his monkey some mean tricks: it started throwing stones at passers-by. If the passer-by happened to be a woman, it would touch its genitals in a lewd manner, take its tiny hands to its nose and sniff at them quickly before covering its face with its hands in mock shame. With every nasty trick performed, Tibo's uncle rewarded the monkey with a banana or some other treat.

From then on, whenever we trespassed in the family's yard to get at the ripe peaches (or was it guavas?) dangling invitingly from their tree's branches, the monkey chased us like an enraged dog. Tibo's uncle continued to reward it with treats for its loyalty to him.

But things got out of hand one day when the monkey viciously clawed a child. Alarmed, Tibo's uncle got rid of his pet. Adults nodded knowingly, as if to say: 'We told you. Monkeys cannot be trusted. You can teach them tricks, but with the promise of more bananas they tend to go beyond the call of duty in their expression of loyalty to their master.'

A chance remark by a friend this week — that this country is becoming a banana republic — brought this lesson learnt from Tibo's uncle's monkey into sharp relief.

Some people have called it a soap opera, but what happened at the SABC this week was monkey business of the lowest order in my terms.

A quick synopsis: two days after the ANC's elective conference in the city of Polokwane, President Mbeki made public the names of new SABC board members, irking the ANC, which had raised questions about the manner in which the board was appointed.

The insinuation was that Mbeki wanted a board that would do his bidding in the fierce fight for the hearts and minds of South Africans. Remarkably, there were neither unions nor representatives from the youth movement on the new board. The inclusion of three specific names had the ANC up in arms: lawyer Christine Qunta, Andile Mbeki and businesswoman Gloria Serobe. By contrast, businessman Peter Vundla was a favourite among all parties concerned.

As soon as the new board assumed its duties, tough questions were asked about the performance of CEO Dali Mpofu — this reportedly coming from the corporation's head of news, Snuki Zikalala. Then board chairman Kanyisiwe Mkonza filed a memo criticising Mpofu.

Last week, the Parliamentary Portfolio Committee on Communications tried to pass a motion of no confidence in the new board. Subsequent confrontations within the ANC's communications study group led to the temporary blocking of the proposed motion. More is reportedly expected to happen this week.

Just watch your TV screen ... oops, you might want to reconsider.

Anyway, while the infighting continued within the ANC, Mpofu, who had long seen the writing on the wall, decided to strike first by suspending Zikalala, who was rumoured to be the board's preferred candidate for the position of CEO.

Hours after Mpofu's pre-emptive strike, the board suspended Mpofu himself.

At the time of writing, we are sitting with a public broadcaster which is rudderless in a country that is supposed to have a vibrant, independent media.

A board that is supposed to be cool headed, well reasoned and thorough in its deliberations is behaving like Tibo's uncle's monkey, which decided to go beyond the call of duty in its expression of loyalty to its master. Did it have to come to this, in a country where we have warned repeatedly of the centralisation of power and the Zanufication of our politics, of the manipulation of our public broadcaster for political gains?

Where are ordinary consumers of news — trying to make sense of the confused and confusing politics of their country — supposed to turn when the public broadcaster becomes a microcosm of monkeydom?

To their credit, senior executives at the SABC have sent a memorandum asking the board to rescind its suspension of Mpofu, or face a walkout that could paralyse the broadcaster. Now some of these members of management who have threatened to resign are consummate professionals whose loyalty lies with the viewer and the listener. If and when they resign, who will do the work, who will create the theatre of the mind for us, who will beam pictures of international developments into our living rooms?

Ah, light-bulb moment: Tibo's uncle's monkey could dust up his CV. Some bananas and nuts might soon be on offer at the public broadcaster.

11 May 2008

I Wanna Sex You Up!

A SCRIBE ONCE WROTE in the now-defunct Staffrider literary magazine that some brands of booze, when you consume them, first make you jocose (you make a fool of yourself, spouting offensive things you mistake for jokes), then bellicose (you grow an unwieldy belly that gets in the way), then comatose (you become uselessly drunk and collapse). I've embellished these thoughts, of course. Can't be trusted to reproduce them verbatim, it was such a long time ago.

Let me use this analogy to tell a summarised version of the history of the IFP (Inkatha Freedom Party).

Growing up in an area dominated by Inkatha in Hammarsdale, I remember supporters of this organisation turning famous church hymns into eulogies to Mangosuthu Buthelezi. 'Imisebenzi kaJesu iyamangalisa (Jesus's works are so wondrous)' became 'Imisebenzi kaShenge iyamangalisa (Shenge's works are so wondrous)' — Shenge, for the uninitiated, is Buthelezi's clan name.

Even as a child I wondered what kind of booze my Inkatha neighbours had consumed to equate Buthelezi with Jesus. I suppose that was the jocose stage of the IFP's genesis.

Then it became bellicose; it was so big (or so it thought) and so consumed with itself that it could not read the changing political landscape.

And then — wham! — the apartheid edifice that had propped it up collapsed and it fell. Comatose.

Now someone has whispered to the IFP that there is a solution, an antidote to the brew that rendered it comatose.

The antidote entails Inkatha launching a beauty pageant, a first for a political party. Desperate times call for desperate measures; measures euphemistically called innovation.

The IFP's 57 constituency areas in KwaZulu-Natal have until September to choose their top 10 contestants for the pageant, the Sowetan reports. The contest is open to women between the ages of 16 and 25.

'By interacting with the youth on a fun level, we are hoping to improve their participation in the electoral process,' the IFP's Sipho Mbatha, the organising brain behind the pageant, is quoted as saying.

Now, I'm not one of those politically correct types who see beauty pageants as cattle parades; I'm all for the celebration of the flowers of our nation. I'm so in love with the concept of beauty that if I were not so aesthetically challenged I would have entered all the Mr South Africa pageants. Alas, the gods were on a go-slow strike when I was conceived.

However, the many beauty pageants I have attended tried not only to celebrate the beauty of the entrants, but also to probe their intellectual prowess.

At one contest, at Diakonia Centre in Durban, a judge probed a contestant's intellectual inclinations: 'What is your favourite dish?'

Contestant: 'Tupperware.'

Judge: 'What do you want to do after school?'

Contestant: 'Homework.'

Since the IFP wants to test the political knowledge of the contestants, I imagine a judge asking: 'Who was the first president of the IFP?'

Contestant: 'Prince Mangosuthu Buthelezi.'

Judge: 'And who was the second?'

Contestant: 'Prince Buthelezi.'

Judge: 'Who delivered the longest speech in the world – longer than Fidel Castro's?'

Contestant (scratching head, biting her nails): 'Prince Buthelezi.'

Ho-hum, this is not working.

Judge (sighing): 'Who was the first chief minister of KwaZulu?'

Contestant: 'Prince Mangosuthu Buthelezi.'

Judge: 'The first minister of police of that territory?'

Contestant: 'Prince Mangosuthu Buthelezi.'

Judge: 'And who was the first minister of finance of that territory?'

Contestant: 'Prince Mangosuthu Buthelezi.'

Judge: 'The name of the main highway in Umlazi?'

Contestant (impatient now): Mangosuthu Highway ...

Judge: 'Aha, gotcha! It's Griffiths Mxenge.' (Judge, to himself: 'Damn!')

I started off dissing the IFP as a comatose party clutching at the skirts of young women to get back on its feet, but I now realise that it is onto something great.

What springs to mind are fresh beginnings for more of the country's challenged political entities, and politicians whose names have been dragged in the mud.

We could start by staging Miss Godzille ('for a friendlier, kinder opposition'); Miss Kanga ('a well- oiled machine; we don't skirt the issues'), Miss Oilgate ('we live off the fat of the land').

I am beginning to appreciate what that kwaito singer was trying to say when he sang: 'Anginamali, anginafoni, anginamoto, anginathenda, kodwa ngiphethe iwewe (I don't have money, don't have a cellphone, don't have a car, don't have a tender, but I've got sex).'

Yep, our politics needs an overhaul; a sexy one if we can help it. Sex sells.

22 May 2007

Snakes Alive! It's enough to make you spit

THE SNAKE IS A HUMBLE BUT SADLY MISUNDERSTOOD and abused creature. Unlike the lion it cannot roar to declare its power and might. Because it slithers and crawls about, it cannot proclaim its majestic power and valour like the ferociously fast cheetah.

It doesn't have limbs, poor thing. It doesn't even have a sense of hearing, for crying out aloud.

The snake is humble. It eats vermin and dust. It can't chew, and thus enjoy its meal, it just ingests. And, having consumed its meal, it must lie uncomfortably for some time while digestion takes place.

Yes, many snakes do have fangs and lethal venom but, in most cases, these are only for self-defence and predatory purposes. The creature is so ineffective that, unlike some mammals and birds, it cannot even make its own shelter. It cannot take care of its young ones. It's significantly insignificant.

And yet, in human mythology, it is painted most unfairly. In the Scriptures, the snake is not only the purveyor of wrongdoing, it is the originator of sin.

It is the snake, the Bible tells us, that led Eve into cajoling Adam into eating the sacred fruit at the centre of the Garden of Eden, provoking God's fury and wrath.

One wonders why the scribes chose the snake as the epitome of wrongdoing. Why not the hyena, for example? After all, it's dirty and ugly enough. Why not a jackal, which, for those who grew up in rural areas, has proved to be a very sly animal?

In conventional speech, when we speak of people with a disagreeable character, we often describe them as slimy snakes.

When we speak of liars, we invoke the snake's forked tongue — yet it cannot even speak. The creature is so disadvantaged that it has to use its tongue for its sense of smell and direction!

Why write volumes of lies about a creature that wouldn't recognise a pen even if it were beaten with it?

In our political lexicon the snake has been brought alive, hissing and writhing under the spotlight.

In the wake of Jacob Zuma's court victory in Pietermaritzburg, in which Judge Chris Nicholson ruled that the decision to prosecute him on corruption and fraud charges was invalid, the ANC president invoked the snake.

In what many perceived to be a reference to Thabo Mbeki, Zuma asked his supporters to stop beating a dead snake.

For the record, this was just days before the ANC recalled Mbeki from his office as president of the republic.

So, in the spirit of the moment, the poetically gifted Zuma told his supporters: 'This time, in particular, you have an opportunity … there's an administration coming to an end, so if you do so [continue attacking the administration that's going] unjengomuntu oshaya inyoka esifile, ubhizi uyayishaya inyoka ife kudala, uyayishaya kodwa (it is like you are beating a snake that is long dead. You are wasting your energy).'

As expected, there were complaints from some quarters about the imagery used. My objection, if I'd been brave enough to lodge it then, would have been from my In Defence of the Poor Snake premise. Why equate the poor, hapless snake with a powerful administration that failed to deliver on its mandate?

Anyway, predictably, ANC Youth League leader Julius Malema was waiting in the wings to defend.

He stretched the imagery even further: 'Fine, we are leaving this dead snake. But we must bury it, it is dead now … we are no longer beating it and we are burying this snake this weekend.'

For some time I laboured under the illusion that the angry hisses about snakes were over — until Zuma invoked the snake once again last week as the battle for the hearts and minds of the South African electorate swung into top gear between the ANC and the rebels who have changed their names three times already — South African Democratic Congress, South African National Congress, and now Congress of the People. There's still uncertainty about this latter name, as the ANC is challenging it. What next? South Africans United in Schizophrenia?

Addressing an audience in the Free State about his new rival Mosiuoa Lekota, Zuma said about the one with the missing tooth: 'Remember, a snake will, from time to time, shed dead skin and leave it behind. The same snake comes out on the other end glowing and looking new. It is the dead skin that you see on TV trying to mislead you.'

In this new rendition of the snake story it was the ANC that was the snake, and Lekota and his acolytes were only the shed skin. Hhawu, this narrative is getting as unwieldy as an anaconda.

So, now the ANC is the snake, and the rebels are the shed skin. Fine.

Then this past Sunday, gwiqiqi — as we say in my language to express a sudden turn of events — Zuma told us that Lekota and his crowd were the snakes.

He said he was happy that the snakes had come out in the open, and the ANC no longer had to worry about 'looking for snakes under its jacket'.

Who is the snake here now? Or, rather, to add an unfortunate sting to the imagery, who is the snake oil merchant here?

Or, who killed the snake so he could obtain its oil, which could then be sold to unsuspecting would-be voters?

Who is speaking with a forked tongue? How did the shed skin of the snake suddenly come back to life?

Ah, the imagery, the imagery! Leave the snake alone, and find some other animal to use as your battering ram.

9 November 2008

The plots just keep thickening

WE'VE GOT LOTS OF PLOTS FOR SALE. Everywhere you turn, you will find a plot. Do you want it on Shaiky ground or do you want it in Tokyo?

Do you want it from Mathews Phosa, or do you prefer Jacob Zuma? Do you want it from the National Intelligence Agency, or would you rather go with Eduardo dos Santos?

Maybe you want it from Terror Lekota? If Terror terrifies you, perhaps you want it from Blade Nzimande. Then again, maybe the Blade is too sharp for you ... gosh, I'm breathless at the number of plots I could mention.

All these plots started surfacing in 2001 when it was alleged that the three musketeers, in the persons of Mathews Phosa, Tokyo Sexwale and Cyril Ramaphosa, had plotted to oust President Thabo Mbeki – their long-standing comrade and colleague in the ruling party's decision-making body, the National Executive Committee. The source of this allegation was Steve Tshwete, one of Mbeki's trusted lieutenants.

Of course, the three ran to the mountaintops, whence they shouted for all to hear that they had no plot whatsoever. In fact, Sexwale even went to the extent of saying that he was through with politics.

Then, in no particular order, other plots started to surface: there was an NIA plot against Saki Macozoma, whose movements were monitored by those of the cloak-and-dagger profession, although why they plotted against him was never established.

The plot began to thicken when Zuma was fired from his job as deputy president of the country.

That was the beginning of the long and winding tale of the Zuma plot. His supporters couldn't understand why the president had fired the man, so they started an interesting, somewhat entertaining, campaign that, in simple terms, told the nation, or whoever cared to listen, that there was an anti-Zuma, and therefore anti-Zulu, plot being hatched by powerful personages in the Union Buildings.

The plot against Zuma began to fester into a series of subplots that boggled the mind.

When Kangaman (Zuma's nickname) appeared in court to face allegations of rape, his supporters initially denied that sex had taken place between him and his accuser.

But when he, himself, confessed that consensual sexual relations had been facilitated in the privacy of his house one night, his supporters changed their tune and said the woman was a pawn in the plot against their leader.

When Schabir Shaik was arrested for his corrupt conduct there was a clamour from the Zuma camp: 'You see, we told you — the system is dealing so harshly with Shaik simply because of his friendship with Zuma.'

And then, not so long ago, we learnt of a plot to assassinate Zuma — although the most cursory investigation showed us that this allegation was groundless. A Zuma aide had paid some hobo to say he had been paid to assassinate Zuma. Confused? So am I.

Then Tokyo, who told us in 2001 that he was out of politics for good, came back into the picture, a player, yet again, in another plot.

This time around he was said to have contacted Zuma to help him elbow (surprise, surprise) Cyril Ramaphosa out of the ANC's presidential race. Zuma was reported to have been outraged by Sexwale's suggestion.

Of course, Sexwale denied the existence of the alleged plot against his former comrade in the alleged plot against Mbeki.

Numerous times Sexwale told the nation that he had no ambition to be president of this country. But then again — gwiqiqi, as we say in Zulu — he joined the presidential race in a big way.

Later there was the smaller matter of him giving his friends and comrades the famous Batho Bonke shares, worth millions.

It was, perhaps, coincidental that the recipients of his largesse were strategically placed individuals like judges, journalists and public commentators.

It was, perhaps, also coincidental that the largesse was extended at a time when the presidential race began in earnest. Do I smell a plot here?

And now we get to the big plot, one of which John le Carré would have been proud. The Sunday Times was the first to reveal, not so long ago, that a document which purports to have been compiled by our respectable spies alleges that, in 2005, Angolan President Eduardo dos Santos appointed his spy boss, General Fernado Miala, to identify 'ways in which Angola could provide support to ... Zuma, and further his presidential aspirations'.

The document further reveals that, during visits to Libya in late 2005, Zuma met

Libyan leader Muammar Gaddafi, or Brother Leader's external intelligence chief, Musa Kusa (why does this name sound so Zulu?), and allegedly received $5-million. 'The purpose of this donation was allegedly ... in support of Zuma's presidential campaign,' the document says.

The name of Blade Nzimande, the general secretary of the South African Communist Party, was mentioned in connection with the plot.

Of course, all the alleged players have dismissed the idea of a plot and have suggested that the insinuations emanate from the Union Buildings. Get it?

But, hey, what's a democracy without a plot?

3 June 2007

I don't get this monk-ey business

EVERYONE IS THROWING THEIR CHOPSTICKS OUT OF THE COT, bickering about the Dalai Lama being denied a visa by South Africa to attend a peace conference which would look at ways of using soccer to fight racism and xenophobia ahead of the 2010 Soccer World Cup.

Moral platitudes about this country's warm relations with China, and therefore its implied lack of commitment to human rights, are flying faster than Bruce Lee's kung fu chops.

I don't get it. What is everybody so excited about?

I have my reasons why I think the Dalai Lama wouldn't have been welcome here.

In South Africa, in our never-ending celebration of 'rainbowism', both the Chinese and African blacks are afforded the same status. They are beneficiaries of affirmative action and black economic empowerment. In a word, they are black.

The relationship runs even deeper between the Chinese and the Zulus — neither can pronounce their Rs.

They are also famous for what many other nations do not really regard as a virtue — fighting skills. So, the Chinese are comfortably black in South Africa.

Now you get a cheeky Chinese fellow who refuses to be part of China, and you think he is going to be welcome here?

He is basically a coconut — a black person who is denying his blackness. In any case, the man doesn't even eat pap and vleis, so what does he want here? Our Chinese friends from Cyrildene and other Chinatowns around the country not only eat skoppo (sheep's head), they also play fah-fee. That's why that game of chance, which has been played in townships for more than six decades, has a Zulu name — umshayina.

The Dalai Lama wouldn't know umshayina if it were to give him a kung fu kick in the face.

The other less reported, but glaringly obvious, reason for the refusal of the Dalai Lama's visa is that at the shindig he was to attend in South Africa, there would have been an over-supply of Nobel peace prize winners — Archbishop Desmond Tutu, Nelson Mandela and F W de Klerk.

Ag, we have enough of our own Nobel winners. Why allow a bald oke from the back of beyond to come and steal the limelight from our own homegrown Nobellers?

And then there's the little matter of the Brits telling us that whenever we want to travel to their miserable, cold little island, we will need a visa.

That pissed us off. We have every right, then, to get somebody pissed off in return.

It reassures us that, like a cock who can strut on his dunghill, we haven't lost everything.

We can diss this cheeky Chinese guy who is refusing to be Chinese. I don't get it. He is Chinese. Or will soon be.

Ask the Taiwanese. They are beginning to dance to the tune of mainland China.

This is realpolitik, people, not some chicken chop suey. And if you think I'm joking, let me strip this matter of all manner of sophisticated nuances. That is the job of the professors and commentators — to 'problematise' a situation, as columnist Xolela Mangcu describes it.

Yet I am a simple man, with a simple take on life — so I will give it to you straight: you are my neighbour, and I give you a loan for your taxi fare — and the next thing I see you having a beer with Mkhize, my arch enemy who is bewitching me, who is sending bolts of lightning to my house!

Hhayi-khona, I won't take that lying down. I will leave you to continue your friendship with Mkhize, and tell you never to come back to me when you need a loan for your taxi fare.

For a long time, the US, at its most arrogant, would say that if you consorted with its enemies, you were therefore an enemy of the US. Unfortunately, that's how power manifests itself. Realism, my friends, realism.

Look, it's not as if we don't like the Dalai Lama. He has, in fact, visited this country twice before. It's not as if he's persona non grata.

Personally, I like the Dalai Lama. The metrosexual dude that I am appreciates his colour co-ordination. But South Africa's trade relations and diplomatic ties are certainly more important than the Dalai Lama's colourful threads.

Let me go further: Sino-French relations soured after French President Nicolas Sarkozy met the Dalai Lama in Poland last year, despite strong protests from China.

In response, China called off the Sino-EU summit scheduled for that month in Lyon, France.

It also cancelled high-level Chinese officials' visits to the country. Premier Wen Jiabao skipped France during his European tour earlier this year.

So, at the end of the day, France is faced with the embarrassing prospect of sending, cap in hand, several high-ranking officials to China next month in an attempt to repair relations between the two countries.

Lento isobala njengempahla yembuzi — this is so obvious even Stevie Wonder, Babsy Mlangeni and Ray Charles (bless his soul) can see it.

The South African government looked at this situation from a practical rather than an emotional perspective. It weighed up the interests of the country, against its understandably important commitment to an international human rights culture.

It's a catch-22 situation. Historically, we are indebted to the international community for their support of our struggle, and the universally expressed abhorrence of a lack of human rights in apartheid South Africa. But at the same time, we should be wary of endangering our ties with China.

My sense is that to avoid the embarrassment, the South African government should have taken a more proactive stance and approached the Dalai Lama with a view to his not making himself available for the peace summit in the first place. The PR disaster is of our government's making.

No, I am no defeatist, nor am I an apologist for our government. I am a realist.

You say South Africa doesn't have balls? I think we do. We're just not ready to lose them — not to a Samurai sword, anyway. Wait a minute, Samurai is Japanese.

Whatever they use to crunch balls out there in Shanghai, South Africa is not ready for it. So, for now, we just have to play ball. The Chinese are the new US, quite frankly.

We've always played ball with the Americans, so what's new? Look, I am a pragmatist. My only regret about Chinese ascendancy is that at my age, I will have to learn yet another new language, Mandarin — just when I was getting confident about English wordplay.

(With a nod to Kaya FM's Phat Joe.)

29 March 2009

Urban Brew

A GOOD BULLY, LIKE A GOOD GAMBLER, knows when to stop. He will accost you on a street corner, kick you around, demand money from you. If you don't have any, he will kick you around some more, chase you down the street, up the road, and stop at the gate to your house.

He will definitely stop.

Now, a bad bully will chase you into your yard, into the kraal where you used to keep your cattle before he took them by force, and throw you to the ground, kicking dusty remnants of cow dung into your face.

At this stage, you snap: Enough! And you surprise the bad bully when you throw him to the ground and proceed to pummel him into a pulp.

The bully I am writing about today comes in all guises and colours; it's multi-headed — omnipotent, almost. I empathise with my good friend Dan Roodt from Dainfern and his disciple, Steve Hofmeyr, who are fighting the bully, protecting their language and cultural rights.

When my people within the labour movement tried to protect workers' rights, the bully labelled them ultra-leftists, counter-revolutionaries. The neo-colonial bully took away our RDP (Reconstruction and Development Programme) and replaced it with Gear (Growth, Employment and Redistribution).

Inasmuch as my people are in love with gears — after all, they drive taxis — they know a bad gear when they see one, and this Gear has resulted in many jobs being lost. At the same time, the neo-colonial hegemony is making my people who have lost their jobs vacate hostels.

Our love for hostels is an accident of history, but we have turned the hostels into vibrant communities, with Block M being occupied by the Mchunu clan from Msinga, and Block D being occupied by the Dhlomos — to avoid faction fights over territory, you see.

The bully hits us, we give him the other cheek. Just when we think he has had enough, he visits upon us yet another indignity.

Taxis are the last outpost in my people's economic survival, but the bully wants to take these away through the Taxi Recapitalisation Programme.

The bully has tried to make it sound fancy, but all it means is that many in the taxi industry are going to lose out, big time.

While we were still trying to make peace with this new insolence from the bully, he has given the SPCA the power to question our right to slaughter our own bulls, in our own hostels, using our own spears. Yaze yasinonela nansi ingulube bo! (This pig is getting too fat for us!).

This week I learnt that the bully is up to his sneaky ways again. He wants to ban umqombothi, our traditional beer, one that has stood the test of time.

It was there long before Charles Glass, the legendary founding brewer of the nation's most famous beer, Castle, was even born.

And while we are at it, I am reminded that just the other day many of my people were wearing red and white, brandishing roses in celebration of one St Valentine, the so-called god of romance. Lies! Indoctrination! Brainwashing! Ah, getting worked up … but yes, a prophet gets laughed at when he's telling the truth.

Back to umqombothi. The International Agency for Research on Cancer has done a study that allegedly shows there are high levels of fungi that are possible cancer-causing agents, or carcinogens, in the homemade brew. (When they use words such as carcinogens, you know you're being had. Big words hide the truth.)

This campaign began a long time ago when the then-government decided to open its own breweries to produce a fake version of the brew, ladled with dollops of chemicals that induced fear for authority on the part of the consumer.

The government had its mad scientists to take care of this process. Wouter Basson wasn't one of them.

The children had no choice but to burn down the government-run beer halls in 1976 in an attempt to jolt their parents into an awareness of reality.

The parents were angry that their children, the contumelious nincompoops, were forcing them to face the harsh reality of life in this country when all they wanted to do was to continue their zombie-like existence.

Anyway, after the uprising the parents became more responsible, and the people started brewing the real umqombothi again, and the community lived happily ever after. You won't find this in history books, thanks to the bully.

Now they want to take the brew away from us. What are they going to do next? Ban mampoer? Ban biltong? Remember the pastor who wrote: 'First they came for the Jews and I did not speak out because I was not a Jew. Then they came for the communists and I did not speak out because I was not a communist … Then they came for me and there was no one left to speak out for me.'

I am writing this on behalf of my brethren who swear by umqombothi. Personally, it gives me heartburn. Makes me fat, makes my hair grow too fast, gives me halitosis. Give me a Johnnie Walker Black or Glenmorangie any time … especially if you are a pale human person or a horizontally challenged, previously disadvantaged Black Economic Empowerment type and you're paying. But, yes, a good bully knows when to stop.

18 February 2007

Where were you when they came for the children?

MANY PEOPLE REMEMBER WHERE THEY WERE, and what they were doing, when they heard about the murder of Prime Minister Hendrik Verwoerd.

Others remember in crisp detail what the weather was like when they learnt of Steve Biko's murder.

Personally, I remember what I was doing when 9/11 was beamed to our TV screens. Having knocked off early from work I was sitting in my lounge, with the TV on, volume off. I was engrossed in Nelson DeMille's The Lion's Game, an airport novel about Libyan 'terrorists' descending on the US.

I kept glancing at the TV screen, seeing these planes plunging into these two tall buildings. What a boring movie this is, I said to myself, and went back to my novel.

Only after my wife phoned and told me to tune in to the TV did I realise that all along I had been watching live footage — and repeats of the same footage — of the fall of the Twin Towers.

This week television and radio stations have been awash with stories of what people were doing, or where they were, when the Soweto uprising of June 16 1976 exploded.

There are many anecdotes, some just bare facts, others thought-provoking vignettes embellished with colour, a bit of exaggeration, a bit of self-deprecating humour. But many of the accounts contradict each other as people, in their own versions, want to place themselves as close to the action as possible.

And there is, of course, a political contest over who started it all. Was it at the instigation of the ANC in exile, or was it just an organic revolt by pupils fed up with inferior education?

What role did the Black Consciousness movement play? Does it matter at all who lit the fuse, so to speak?

These are questions being grappled with in a slew of books that have been published as we commemorate the 30th anniversary of this momentous occasion.

I guess what I am saying is that, in our individual recollection of the past, we sometimes distort history so we can have a place in it, so we can be actors in it, purveyors of the freedom that we enjoy today.

But the reality is that we couldn't all have been soldiers at the forefront of the struggle.

There were the stone-throwers and the martyrs; there were observers — of a professional nature, like journalists, and just plain pedestrian observers. As Arthur Nortje said in his poem 'Native's Letter': 'For some of us must storm the castles/ some define the happening.'

Personally, I don't remember the day of June 16 1976 per se. I was only nine, going on 10, and living in a small township in the heartland of KwaZulu-Natal, far from the madding crowd.

But, like the rest of the country, a few days after the fateful day our small township did undergo some change.

My first recollection is that we were in joyous spirits when the teachers told us to go home, and stay away from school until we were called back. Wow! Jolly good, an unexpected holiday! We could go and play marbles, fish the dirty streams on the outskirts of the township and, when bored with it all, pull out our slingshots and start surreptitiously breaking neighbours' windows, as was the fashion.

But then the parents and the teachers put their foot down: while you are away from school, no venturing outdoors, they said.

There were morbid whispers about children disappearing mysteriously. Something, some force, was snatching them away.

Soon, the kidnapping campaign was given a name: Phungukani MaZulu — we are reducing the number of Zulus.

It was said that Phungukani MaZulu had magic. The Phungukani MaZulu car could change itself into a frog, a vegetable, an insect, before its occupants got out and snatched an unsuspecting child. Wherever they went, children had to be vigilant. And one Saturday morning as I walked home from the nearby shop, Phungukani MaZulu came for me.

I heard a sound in the road, and turned to see an onion rolling in my direction. My mind screamed: Phungukani MaZulu! I ran.

Neighbours shouted, why was I screaming and running?

'Phungukani MaZulu is chasing after me! Help! Help!'

Sweating, I rushed into our home, locking the door behind me.

Even though my mother tried to reassure me that Phungukani MaZulu didn't exist, that it was a scare story to keep children indoors, she didn't sound convinced herself. For a start, she couldn't explain the disappearance of some children from their homes.

Decades later, with the benefit of hindsight, and having studied history, I realised that the disappearances were linked to the wave of radicalism that followed the Soweto uprising, when scores of children fled into exile, or were detained without trial.

That's my recollection of 1976: not the day itself, but the thorns that grew in its wake, thorns we had to brave as we soldiered ahead into the future.

My hope is that my children and their children will succeed in removing from this nation's heart the thorns of bitterness and hatred.

Let them enjoy the fruit of our labour, the fruit that's beckoning on the horizon, asking to be plucked and cherished.

18 June 2006

Dropped on his head as a baby, and about to be dropped again

I WAS HOPING THAT THE BOERHAHA over ET's death would have died down by now - but, no, our papers are not giving us a respite, bombarding us as they do with daily, if not hourly, new revelations about what really happened on the day Mr Blowtorch Eyes was killed.

To save its puritanical, holier-than-thou face, the AWB is trying hard to distance ET from the lurid allegations of what, if it were to be made into a movie, would be called One Leader, One Smirnoff, One Condom, Two Darkies en 'n Klomp Savannahs.

With every detail, we cringe and shout indignantly that we've had enough - only to "ooh" and "aah" as we lap up another revelation on our front pages. Scandal is addictive.

ET's supposed touchy-feely tendencies were given a whole new context by the new AWB leader, Andre Visagie, and his obsession with e.tv anchorman Chris Maroleng's studio.

I mean, the country was holding its collective breath, waiting for Visagie to say something sensible about what ET's death meant for the future of race relations in this country - but, no, Visagie was having none of the race-relations stuff. All he was interested in was touching Maroleng on his studio.

Maroleng had to cry out a number of times, "Don't touch me on my studio!"

But, like a jilted lover who won't take no for an answer, Visagie crooned: "I will touch you on your studio."

Maybe Maroleng should consider putting barbed wire around his studio. That way Visagie will refrain from his touchy-feely tendencies when it comes to the man's studio. AWB types have great respect for barbed wire.

Having dispensed with those touchy-feely tendencies of the AWB types, I thought I should take the debate about our nationhood to a new and higher intellectual plain.

Where I come from, you don't kick a man when he is down - even if he has proved to be a rapscallion of unremitting delinquency. What you do is get the beaten man gently back on his feet, pat him soothingly on his shoulder and politely ask after his health.

If he says he is fine, you hit him very hard again and let him drop like a sack of potatoes to the ground. When he is down, you get him back on his spindly legs. And you repeat the process.

Ah, it can get highly addictive, this act of helping a hapless person onto his feet ...

only to pummel him to the ground. It's a very civilised way of dealing with contumelious nincompoops, too. Especially those who won't listen to reason, those who were dropped on their heads when they were young. These who were dropped on their heads, as long-standing readers of this column will remember, are called amahlongandlebe (ihlongandlebe, singular).

Because they were dropped on their heads in childhood, they are quite used to hard knocks on the noggin. In fact, they are immune to hard knocks.

It requires the patience of Job to perfect this skill of dealing with children who were dropped on their heads.

After some practice, President Jacob Zuma is showing signs that he is getting the hang of it: every time Juju Man spoils his pants in public, Zuma knocks him down viciously, only to pick him up and give him one of those signature smiles … before dropping him with another punch.

For some time, many of us thought Zuma was scared of Juju; that he was treating him with kid gloves. Careful observation and analysis are beginning to tell me that Zuma has finally learnt how to deal with the Dropped-On-Their-Heads brigade. I hope my diagnosis is correct.

When Juju was in the news last week about his alleged ill-treatment of a BBC journaist, the ANC issued what sounded like a cosy statement - distancing itself from Juju Man, but not quite willing to denounce him outright. And just when Juju thought everything was okay, that the comrades had cleaned his nappies for him once again, JZ came with a punch that dropped the poor youth leader to the ground. The president even called Juju's behaviour "alien".

"But I was born in Limpopo," Juju Man complained. "How can I be called an alien!" Juju Man's somewhat-educated imbongi, Floyd Chihuahua, explained to his boss that "there's a difference between an alien and being alien … um, ah, the intricacies of the queen's language, comrade, um, ah, you can be alien without being an alien, I'm not quite sure either, comrade, but the English language is very complex …"

For the first time, Juju looked bewildered: how could his beloved father drop him like that? And even call him an alien?

In desperation, Juju tried a not-so-new trick: blame the media. He said he had not meant to call BBC journalist Jonah Fisher a bastard. In fact, said he, he had thought the journalist's name was Ted. So, as a well-brought-up Pedi boy who respects white people, he had thought it proper to address the white journalist from overseas as "Baas Ted". The Facebook tribe had a good laugh at Juju's lame attempt.

Then Juju instructed Floyd Chihuahua to try another trick.

So the imbongi Chihuahua dispatched a statement which stated, among other things, that "counter-revolutionary ailments within the media were casting aspirations upon the president of the youth league", blah, blah.

But the statement only deepened the crisis: the office of the secretary-general of the ruling party wanted to know about Juju's declared "aspirations". Was he suffering from the well-known ailment called ambition? Was he having "aspirations" to take over the secretary-general's office? Was he having "aspirations" to take over the office of the deployment commissar so he could have a more hands-on role in the issuing of government tenders?

Once again, Juju was floored.

But there were already noises that when the president of the country came back from his trip to Brazil, he would pick Juju Man up, only to drop him once again with a vicious right hook.

This time Juju is facing disciplinary measures from the top dogs of the ruling party.

If I were Juju Man, I would just play dead.

But, damn, you can't tell with the One Who Was Dropped On His Head

18 April 2010

I'd like a word, Floyd - kno' what I'm sayin'?

When I was barely in my teens I, like many of my peers, was energetic, ambitious and imaginative - imaginative to the extent that I thought I had the power, the talent and the vision to change the world: the soccer world, the literary world, the music world, the world of political activism.

I was a regular feature in one of my province's colourful soccer sides (albeit owned by and run for my father). I wrote some poems which my friends thought were brilliant. I sang in my church choir (but they cleverly prevented me from taking tenor solos). And I could quote the Steve Bikos of this world at the drop of a hat.

In mid-high school my world came crashing down when I suddenly realised that I had been living a lie, and that my parents had been aiding and abetting me in my pursuit of the mirage of fame and fortune.

I was bad at soccer, the poems that I thought were brilliant were torn to shreds by my neighbour Mafika Gwala (the internationally acclaimed poet and activist), and somebody introduced the Shell Road to Fame music talent show - and I didn't even make the provincial leg of the contest.

Thankfully, I was humble and realistic enough to realise that, if I took my own life in the face of these disappointing discoveries, the world would not come to an abrupt halt.

The headline would have read: "Frederick Vusisizwe Khumalo found hanging in his bedroom. No foul play suspected." Who would have cared?

That was when the world was harsh, unforgiving and unsympathetic to emotional fools.

That was when you were not told what you wanted to hear. If you were nothing, that was it. You were simply nothing. Full stop. No platitudes about "hidden talent", "potential", "rough diamond".

I was born in vinegar times and fed with lemons, to quote from Mzwakhe Mbuli's "poem" about those tough times. By the way, where is the Tall Man? Composing another poem? Run for cover.

Anyway, when I came crashing down to terra firma, I had no one to pick me up. I had to stand up on my own, dust the seat of my pants and make peace with the fact that I was not oozing talent.

Maybe my mission on earth was to become a bricklayer. That did cross my mind, once, but having worked in white people's gardens I had realised over the years that I was not cut out for back-breaking labour.

For a fleeting moment I thought I could try my luck at robbing banks. But, hey, it soon dawned on me that I was too lily-livered for that profession.

Common sense dictated that I spend a lot more years at school so I could get a job - even if it meant being a clerk confined to a desk in a government department.

But these days, everyone is a poet, everyone is a musician, everyone is an orator, everyone is an author.

If you, based on past experience, try to politely to nudge the would-be artist out of his reverie and get him or her to think again, you are labelled "part of the conservative, backward establishment", "counter-revolutionary", "coconut apologist for the establishment", a "jealous failure".

I have been called all these - and worse - for merely trying to save the would-be artists the embarrassment guaranteed to follow those who refuse to take a thorough look at their strengths and weaknesses and make the necessary adjustments.

Plunging oneself into a pair of oversized jeans, wearing a golf cap backwards and peppering one's speech with four-letter words and phrases such as "kno'what I'm sayin'?" does not necessarily make an overnight hip-hop sensation. Just because you can switch on a computer and tap something on the keyboard does not make you a writer.

But all of this, which I consider common sense, seems lost on thousands of young - and not so young - people in this country.

When Floyd Shivambu, the ANC Youth League's spokesman, threatened to expose unsavoury aspects of the lives of some journalists - and further called some of them "sick and mentally disturbed" - I was one of the few journos who requested that the young man be forgiven his faux pas.

When you are constantly in the company of Julius Malema, it is easy to get your tongue in a knot. It is easy to think you are a mightily talented orator, thinker, activist, and everything else besides.

So, I asked my colleagues not to be too harsh on poor Floyd; he was but a victim of circumstances. He was Malema's fellow traveller down the road to dangerous self-delusion.

Before I started drafting a short, funny column in defence of poor Floyd, I decided to surf the Net in search of recent utterances by him.

I stumbled upon something called Floetry - Poetry According to Floyd, published under Floyd Shivambu's name, on a website called The New Black Magazine.

Here goes:

I wouldn't write a poem
I wouldn't write a poem to weave love phrases and praises
I would never put a pen on paper to utter how much I love you
Never would I play with words and phrases about love, love and love
I wouldn't say to a paper that you are the jewel of my heart
I would never rave about, eulogise, applause your beauty with ink
Never would I pour my heart through the tip of pen onto a virgin paper
Excuse me, I never write fairly tails about love, love and love
I wouldn't defuse your mentality through printed words and phrases
I never say to the paper blank script how much I love you
I never send black blue ink in red to your heart to speak out my love
I wouldn't put and pour my whole heart into a blank, plain ... void paper
Never would I say to the paper that I love to love you
... But because it's you, never to be reduced to poetic phrases and praises
Pen, paper, and guitar I take,
To declare my love to you on paper, I write a poem

But, no dear reader, the above wasn't just a once-off. There was another piece:

Contemporary Azanian Child
A child of about just over teen years
Strolling the streets of Jozi
Empty stomach, empty handed
Only 5 bucks for a taxi home
Home being a single roomed shack in township house backyard
A child full of unattainable ambitions
Wish I could own a BMW or Benz
Wish I could buy a house in sub-urban Jozi
Wish I could dine and wine from silver plates and cups
Wish I could learn how to use silver spoons, forks and knives

Wish I could wear Guess what? Palazollo pitti and fake Chuck Taylor sneakers
Wish I could just jol a well-shaped, facially gifted lover with class
Wish I could buy chicken feet to feed my empty baseless belly
And also wish to get another 5 bucks for a taxi to Jozi
Maybe I will get a job
Damn!

Damn, Floyd, what was that? I know that they say a prophet is never appreciated in his lifetime. I know poetry shouldn't be read literally. I know that in contemporary South Africa, where everything goes, a lot of people flinch at the mention of the word "standards". But still. Fairly tails? Virgin paper? Blue ink in red? How about you try your hand at word work, Floyd? Maybe you can do better than your comrade Malema.

Floyd, here and now, in front of millions of readers, I withdraw my request that you be forgiven. You have insulted the art of writing. And that is unforgivable. As Justice Malala would say: There must be a law (against this).

This is a crime against humanity, Floyd. A crime, a crime, a crime.

4 April 2010

In Memoriam

Ode to Spencer, the proud kwerekwere

THE FIRST TIME I MET HIM, IN 1997, my friend Spencer Chirambo told me an ironic joke. He said: 'A number of guys are sitting at a bar, drinking, when one of them, a Mozambican, gulps his beer in a hurry and smashes his glass on the floor.

'Everyone in the bar is shocked. They want to know why he's smashing his glass on the floor.

'The Mozambican responds: "Back home in my country, we've got so much unique, top-class sand that we use it to manufacture glass. As a result I don't have to drink from the same glass more than once."

'Then a Nigerian fellow follows suit, smashing his glass on the floor. When asked why he's doing it, he responds: "Back home we've got so much money from our oil riches and from our 419 businesses we don't have to drink from the same glass more than once."

'Looking at all this mayhem, the third guy, a South African, finishes his drink in a hurry, reaches for his gun and shoots his two foreign drinking mates.

'Eish! Everybody ducks for cover. Then the shaken barman pleadingly asks the South African about this act of violence he's just committed.

'The South African tucks his gun into his jacket pocket, and responds calmly: "In South Africa we've got so many makwerekwere I don't have to drink with the same ones more than once."'

That was how Spencer Chirambo told me the story, illustrating our sometimes ridiculous intolerance of foreigners, but I've heard versions of the same tale over the years.

The irony was that Spencer was, himself, a kwerekwere, a Malawian who transplanted himself successfully in South African soil. The word kwerekwere is generally used as an insult — but Spencer wore his kwerekwerehood with pride.

In his self-deprecating style he used to tell us what a clever kwerekwere he was, as he could speak more South African languages than many of us natives of this country.

He knew more places of fun than many of us. He was known to more famous people than many of us. In fact, many people mistook him for a local guy, so encyclopaedic was his knowledge about this country, ranging from its politics to its sports.

I guess I'm retelling this story as a tribute of sorts to Spencer, who died last weekend.

People tell how Spencer watched the Kaizer Chiefs vs Sundowns game from beginning to end on Saturday. Then a few hours later, he started complaining of being cold. He had what appeared to be a heart seizure and died.

People say he couldn't stomach the defeat of his beloved Sundowns. In Africa we laugh in the face of death. Still, it's difficult to come to terms with a sudden death such as Spencer's — especially because he was only in his mid-30s.

Spencer was taken from us by the big disease with a small name, as androgynous singer Prince is said to have called it.

It wasn't so long ago that Spencer told his coterie of friends what was eating him. Of course his revelation came as a shock to many.

But after a few weeks in hospital he was discharged, showing signs of recovery. Soon he was back in the 'hood, telling funny stories.

One of the stories he told just before Christmas was how he had tried to pretend to be an illegal foreigner so that the police could arrest and deport him to his home country, where he could enjoy Christmas with his family in Blantyre, and later come back to South Africa.

But Home Affairs Minister Nosiviwe Mapisa-Nqakula was a spoilsport when she decided not to arrest or deport foreigners over that period, having wised up to the strategy they were using as a way of travelling home at the government's expense.

To their chagrin, the likes of Spencer ended up having Christmas with the likes of us in the unusually quiet and boring surrounds of Johannesburg.

If I wanted to be politically unctuous I would be telling you now that Spencer died of TB, or pneumonia.

But no, I would be lying to you. I would be lying to myself. I would be perpetuating a national lie that says there's a TB epidemic, and not an HIV/Aids epidemic, in this country.

Spencer was brave enough to shrug off the lie and tell the truth that the ogre with a small name was upon him. Why, then, should I betray him by lying to myself; by telling a lie?

Spencer, wherever you are now, remember that the brothers respect you for the stance you took, for telling the truth in the face of all the stigmas attached to the ogre that many of us are afraid to even call by its name.

When the bulk of this nation is in denial, when those in power are whipping us, saying that this ogre is not potent, that in fact it doesn't exist, those in our country who are now at its mercy will continue to die.

All we need is the humility to admit the existence of this ogre in our midst. We also need the political will to deal with it urgently and decisively.

When that happens, people like Spencer will be saved, or their lives prolonged through proper nutrition, medication and counselling.

And writers would not need to tell ironic jokes in an attempt to come to terms with the sadness and the shock of it all.

27 February 2005

Brother, you rocked my world... and my wardrobe

I WEAR PINK SHIRTS. Silk, preferably. And black shoes. Lots of them. And many of them sharp-pointed. Pure leather. White socks galore. The Philistines laughed so much at the white socks that I've decided to stop wearing them. I have a predilection for tight-fitting jeans.

Even at 40-something when the mood takes me I still moon walk, swirling and slithering all over the place; so much so that my kids sometimes think I've put butter on the soles of my shoes. Damn, this is all thanks to Michael Jackson.

I have, on many occasions, written about how the US has insinuated itself into the global psyche — not through its military might, not through flexing its financial muscle, but through its artistic output.

In 1993 funnyman Kinky Friedman wrote the book Elvis, Jesus and Coca-Cola. If he had hailed from my generation, Friedman would have titled his book Michael Jackson, Jesus and Coca-Cola.

Columnist John Nichols has written: 'The better part of a quarter of a century before Barack Obama was credited with remaking America's global image, Michael Jackson presented the US as a country where an African-American kid from Gary, Indiana, could, on the basis of remarkable talent and drive, become fabulously successful, fabulously influential and fabulously wealthy.'

Influential is the operative word for me. When we were young, in the tradition of many black and coloured townships, we had gangs. But the word 'gang' has negative connotations. It evokes images of guns, knives and drugs — so let's call them sub-cultures.

In the white community they have the Goths, in the '80s they had the punk rockers. In the black tradition, we've had the Ivies, the Rastas, the Pantsulas, the American Dudes. I belonged to the latter.

Interestingly enough — apart from the Rasta movement — all the other traditions were influenced by American culture. The music we listened to, the clothes we wore, and even the slang was American — yah dig?

The Ivies were older, more refined. They wore tight-fitting bell bottoms with high-heeled shoes and listened to the O'Jays, the Manhattans and The Temptations,

And we, the young bucks, called ourselves, the American Dudes, yah know what I'm sayin'? When we started out, we wore Bang-Bang stretch jeans and high-heeled shoes and the Afro was the hairstyle of choice.

Later, we permed our hair and used greasy gels, hoping to look like Michael Jackson.

When I was in high school our uniform was supposed to be a white shirt, black tie, grey trousers and black shoes. We respected the tradition — except that instead of the drab and boring Pep Store regulation uniform, we improvised and wore white Georgette shirts, multi-zippered grey pants and high-heeled Watson shoes, Michael Jackson-style.

The school tried to dissuade us from this ostentatious display and some of us threatened to boycott classes. They left us alone — with our greasy perms.

Up to matric I was still wearing my multi-zippered botsotso pants. And we hacked the legs off the pants so we could display our socks — Michael Jackson-style. And we bought fake leather jackets with countless zips. And when some of us reached adulthood and started working we bought genuine leather black jackets — Michael Jackson-style. And we bought pink Pierre Cardin shirts, mauve Yves St Laurent suits and black moccasins — Michael Jackson-style.

When I see my white colleagues wearing Bob Dylan fedora hats or trying to sound as risqué as the Sex Pistols — with all those four-letter words littering every utterance — I fully understand where they are coming from.

You see, there are moments in life — politically, culturally and otherwise — that define us. Sometimes we are not even conscious of these influences, until someone mentions them — or an icon like Michael Jackson dies. And we remember. Oh, do we remember!

For as long as I can remember my colleagues at the Sunday Times have commented on my pink shirts as well as my predilection for orange or yellow jerseys, my red leather jacket and cashmere coats.

Until this week, the Michael Jackson week, I had forgotten where the influence came from. Then I remembered. Oh, did I remember!

Yes, we grow up, and we embrace other forms of artistic expression: Picasso paintings; Sekoto's reproductions of South African life; hollering John Coltrane; the understated Duke Ellington; the sombre Mankunku Ngozi; crazy Fela Kuti; and the haunting jazz genius, Miles Davis. Especially Miles Davis.

Davis is an artist who left an indelible mark on the artistic and literary minds of many. At some stage he also wanted to play and record with Prince and Michael Jackson.

When his attempts to play with Jackson failed Miles did cover versions of some of Jackson's songs, Human Nature being one of them.

Isn't that genius? Tell me, is it not?

They say the kid from Gary, Indiana, never grew up. Maybe he didn't. Maybe he didn't want to. Maybe he knew what 'growing up' entailed. What does it entail? Who knows? They called him Peter Pan, a weirdo, a freak. Yes, they judged him.

However, this man — or boy-child, as some called him — changed the world of music videos with the release of Thriller, a classic by all definitions. Thriller is a movie on its own. Block out the music, put it on mute on your TV and the story remains. It set a standard that many other artists could only hope to emulate.

There are very few pop artists who can sustain their careers beyond five years. Remember how long the Sex Pistols lasted, or the Allman Brothers? Many artists can sell millions in two years, three at most. But few can sustain that hit-after-hit schedule for four decades.

Jackson did, starting in his pre-teen years with his siblings, when he sang his way into the hearts of countless millions all over the world. He earned 13 Grammy awards and 13 No 1 singles as a solo performer, achieving sales in excess of 750-million albums.

Did you hear that?

Even those who couldn't speak English tried their best to sing his catchy songs, which were commentaries on life: 'Black or White'; 'Bad'; 'Dirty Diana'; 'Billie Jean'; Beat It … man, his s*** was cool. Cool and memorable. Danceable too.

When he moonwalked, his energy, his movement, spoke of the unimaginable possibilities of the human mind. Jackson was someone you couldn't ignore, even if you hated him.

Yes, many are bound to hate him because, as human beings, we have short memories. We tend to judge people by their latest foibles or fall from grace.

Yes, like the rest of us, he had his dark side — like, for example, when he tried to alter his nose. Such a decent, good-looking human being trying to be what he was not. What a shame.

And then there were shenanigans with children — his and other people's. But that was later in his life.

The life that I will remember and celebrate will be his fashion sense, his humility and his artistic genius. What a loss to humanity!

Yes, I will continue wearing my pink shirts, Mikey. In memory of you. Farewell, brother.

28 June 2009

John Matshikiza: A Tribute*

THE AMERICAN LITERARY GENIUS, Gore Vidal, once observed that critics 'are fundamentally mechanics. They go about dismantling the text with the same rapture that their simpler brothers experience while taking apart internal combustion engines: inveterate tinkerers both, solemnly playing with what has been invented by others for use, not analysis.'

Now I am standing in front of you in the hope that you will forgive me for trying to be a literary mechanic, and not a good one at that. I have been asked to give a talk on John Matshikiza and his contribution – not only his newspaper column writing, but his broader legacy and lasting impact on the arts. Were he still alive he certainly would have graced this year's National Festival with his rambunctious presence. Alas, he is no longer with us – which is why I have been asked to give this short talk. But more than being a newspaper columnist, Bra John was one of those polymaths that this country has an odd way of producing: film and stage actor, poet, journalist, broadcaster, and political activist – and he seemed equally comfortable in each of these roles.

A year is not over since he died – on September 15 2008 – but the literary mechanic that is me is already trying to tinker with the man's legacy. Those who knew him from his exile days in London will tell you that even though he was from a political family – his father was the great Todd Matshikiza, famous for his Drum magazine columns, but even more famous for writing King Kong, the 1950s musical – John Matshikiza was more comfortable expressing himself artistically than climbing on to the stage to deliver a slogan-riddled political speech.

Many might say he was apolitical, but nothing could be further from the truth. It's just that many of us are more adept at parochial sloganeering, which is, sadly, in most cases confused with political expression. Bra John was more subtle in his exploration of the human condition; preferring to use the arts to drive home political messages.

Born in Johannesburg in 1954, he left South Africa with his parents as a young boy. The Matshikizas' odyssey saw them living in London and, later, Lusaka, Zambia. After his father's death in 1968, Bra John returned to London to study at the Central School of Speech Training and Dramatic Art. After training with the Royal Shakespeare Company he worked for the Glasgow Citizens Theatre Company. In conjunction with the likes of Mandla Langa – now an accomplished novelist – in the 1970s Bra John helped form Mayibuye, the cultural wing of the ANC. He also lived in the US, Amsterdam, and various African countries including Senegal, where he was culture director of the Gorée Institute. Apart from acting, he also directed and wrote for both theatre and television.

When the ANC was unbanned, John Matshikiza was one of the first returnees to take advantage of this momentous occasion. On his return he did some stints at the Market Theatre in Johannesburg, mainly in a directorial role. It was also around this time that he started plying his trade as a columnist with the Sunday Independent.

His column, written in a deft, crisp style, was an eclectic mix of political commentary, occasional nostalgic walks down memory lane and, sometimes, childlike awe-struck observations about this country in which he was born, but which never felt – and would never feel – completely like home. He was too much a man of the world to be confined to some corner of Melville, or Houghton, or Soweto, or KwaMashu, or Gugulethu.

I got this sense of disconnection when I first met him in 1995. I was, at that time, working for a small TV production as a scriptwriter. My boss, Marc Caplan, wanted to do a multi-media project on Drum – the magazine itself and the literary tradition it engendered. Having been introduced we immediately hit it off – the drinks helped a lot – and he was pleasantly surprised that I had read every copy of Drum magazine that I could lay my hands on. At that time the Drum archive was located at the farmhouse of Jim Bailey, the eccentric founder of the magazine.

But when we got down to writing the story John seemed uncomfortable with the approach – and he said as much to me and Caplan. He was too obsessed with the story of his father and wanted to take ownership of it in all its manifestations and at all costs. And although he was a soft-spoken guy, Bra John could stand his ground. As a result of his stubbornness, the Drum project, as envisioned by Caplan never saw light of day.

Years later, when Zola Maseko did a feature film on Drum magazine, Bra John excoriated the young director for ostensibly portraying his father, Todd, as an intellectually challenged coon.

He delivered the same treatment to Ronald Suresh Roberts after the latter recorded, in his biography of Nadine Gordimer, how she had been a benefactor of Todd, bestowing upon him a beautiful piano. Bra John took umbrage at the Trinidadian biographer's tone and insinuation that Todd had been no intellectual but only something of a participant in a colourful carnival that came with working at Drum.

John Matshikiza: A Tribute*

Apart from writing the column in the Sunday Independent John was much in demand on the big screen. His most famous role was in There's a Zulu on my Stoep (1993). He personally reviled the movie – as a serious artist's artist the slapstick comedy of Schuster did not sit well with him – but, hey, he needed to make a living. However, that he executed his role with such a sense of joie de vivre and boisterous confidence proves his mettle and his genius as an artist.

Many other movie roles were to follow, the last one being, if memory serves me well, Hijack Stories (2000), the movie that, to my mind, catapulted actor Rapulana Seiphemo, into the stratosphere. But Bra John also acted in more ambitious works such as Richard Attenborough's Cry Freedom (the 1987 tribute to Steve Biko and Donald Woods) and 1987's Mandela, a made-for-television movie in which he played the role of Walter Sisulu.

So, what was his contribution to newspaper column writing? It is generally said and believed that a good newspaper is a nation talking to itself. With this observation in mind, therefore, I have decided that a good newspaper columnist is a conductor, a purveyor of this national dialogue.

Bra John was good at conducting this dialogue. His subjects ranged from the arts to politics; from sport to race relations. He brought to newspaper column writing his sense of drama. And lots of humour. Bra John came home, as I have said, but with an outsider's eye and heart. He came home at a time when there was that social conflict – understated or undeclared as it was.

There was conflict between the exiles and the inziles. There was conflict over issues ranging from affirmative action to black economic empowerment and their efficacy. He came home when there was conflict in the suburbs, the white, long-established residents of these abodes still trying to make peace with their new black neighbours, who would drop a cow or goat at the slightest provocation.

When white people are having a good time they turn down the music and have a conversation; in the black tradition, when we are having fun, we turn up the volume of the music, and leave conversation for more sombre occasions, such as funerals. Bra John Matshikiza explored all of these contradictions. In one of his columns in the Mail & Guardian he wrote of the irony of South Africa becoming 'the great white hope of the black diaspora … People speak comprehensible English here. Telephones work.

112

There's a black president, a largely black cabinet, black empowerment and a black economic elite, which, even though they may show signs of moral confusion and fallibility, nevertheless symbolise a significant advance in the worldwide profile of the black world.'

Admittedly, there were some occasions when one would be tempted to ask: but why has he decided to write about a funeral? Who does not know what a township funeral is like? But, remember, Bra John was but a child who had come home from a lifetime in exile. And the home he had come to was like a box of chocolates – always full of surprises. As was to be expected, therefore, his columns were always full of surprises. They might be rude, unpleasant, and sometimes infantile surprises, but they were surprises nevertheless.

For unravelling these surprises Bra John earned himself respect as a columnist, winning, in 2002, both the regional and national Vodacom Journalist of the Year Award in the specialist category for his column, which later appeared in a collection of his and his father Todd's works, titled With The Lid Off: South African Insights from Home and Abroad.

Bra John also published collections of work such as "South Where Her Feet Cool on Ice" (1981), and "Prophets in the Black Sky" (1986). When he died, he was busy writing a biography of his father. It was an ambitious project, for which he was granted the coveted Wiser Scholarship. Although he had done a lot of work on the biography, he once told me, he sadly didn't see the project through.

It is my submission, therefore, that it is that childlike sense of wonder that made his columns memorable. Let me hazard a guess that columnists writing today and in future will always be tempted to inhabit Bra John Matshikiza's world of wonder and surprise – through the newspaper column.

* Talk delivered on July 4 2009 at the National Arts Festival, Grahamstown.

5 July 2009

Sex Talk

Degradation in the name of teenage sexual morality

IT IS MY BELIEF THAT ADOLESCENCE is the most truculent period in life (others will say adolescence is but a close second to senility, but I won't enter that debate since I haven't reached the green pastures of old age yet …).

In adolescence we become the most disagreeable creatures on God's Earth: we think we are the cleverest, coolest and strongest beings ever created.

It is during adolescence that many of us plunge into nihilistic behaviour — experimenting with drugs, sex or crime, for example — from which we sometimes never recover.

And, oh, are we adolescents touchy!

It is against the fragile persona of an adolescent that I have always wondered what virginity testing, and other means of monitoring the sexuality of young people, does to the girls subjected to it. A part of the answer to that question came a few weeks ago when I read "Breath, Eyes, Memory", a shocking novel by the Haitian writer Edwidge Danticat.

The narrator of the story is a Haitian girl called Sophie, who, since about the age of 12, has been subjected to virginity testing by her mother, who slides her little finger into the girl's private parts to make sure the hymen is intact.

The mother thinks this is a virtuous and proper way of making her daughter respect her sexuality as she moves into adulthood. After all, such testing had been carried out for generations, not only in her family, but in her section of Haitian society.

Out of this crucible had emerged women who obeyed culture. This was a culture that stipulated that each and every finger on a woman's two hands had a purpose: mothering, boiling, loving, baking, nursing, frying, healing, washing, ironing and scrubbing.

Whenever Sophie has to be tested her mind goes blank and she feels like nothing.

When she finally reaches adolescence and has moved from rural Haiti to the US, where her mother is working, her world view changes, just as her hormones are taking over the way she behaves. In a moment of what many might regard as insanity, the girl fetches a broomstick and plunges it into her essence, breaking her own virginity. It's a powerful yet shocking act of rebellion — against her mother, her culture and her community's expectations of her. Even before reading this book I was opposed to virginity testing, which has been revived in some parts of South Africa. The practice has been hailed by many as a move towards restoring morals among young girls and protecting them against HIV/Aids. Without having said it in so many words, I have thought of virginity testing

117

as demeaning to the girls and insulting to the perpetrator (the examiner). No one can control another person's sexuality without debasing her own integrity. The jailer is often more morally bankrupt than the jailed.

But until reading "Breath, Eyes, Memory", I had never thought of the possible psychological damage testing might do. Some 'victims' play along merrily (at least on the outside) because the testing affirms them in the public eye, making them paragons of morality. But, until one encounters someone like Sophie, one can only wonder at the extent of the psychological damage, conscious or subconscious, done by these virtuous tests. In the book, when Sophie's mother discovers to her shock that her hitherto obedient, morally upright daughter has lost her virginity, she wonders what went wrong. Naturally, she looks into that dark part of her heart where the demons of self-blame reside; then she plunges into the abyss of madness and endless nightmares.

A friend I discussed the book with remarked that the girls who undergo virginity testing are, in fact, luckier than those elsewhere on the continent whose clitorises are cut off and their labia sewn together, leaving only a small hole to pass urine through, as a sure way to suppress their sexual appetites. I groaned at the barbarity of it all. But I still maintained that the South African testing was equally bad in that, while not as crude as mutilation, it could leave scars on the girl's psyche.

I have yet to be confronted with the tragic results of virginity testing in the South African context. I have yet to hear from the horse's mouth what it has done to the psyches of girls who, at regular intervals, have to undress and be examined. I also wonder what happens when the mothers of the hitherto well-behaved girls suddenly discover, at first hand, that their daughters have lost their prized virginity. Imagine the sense of loss, the sense that they have been shown disrespect. It is heartening that the Draft Bill on Children's Rights and Protection outlaws virginity testing. It's about time. Instead of championing the physical testing, parents and others rightly concerned with the chastity of children should be talking more with their daughters about their need to control their sexual urges; to protect themselves from unwanted pregnancies and disease. Sexuality can be managed and negotiated, never controlled. That much we should have learned from the failure of the Immorality Act, which tried to legislate sex lives.

3 July 2005

Covet not thy President's wives...

IN THE BUILD-UP TO JACOB ZUMA'S inauguration the human detritus that I hobnob with at our local watering hole were obsessing about what they called South Africa's new president's polygamous poser: which of his wives was going to be the first lady?

With his inimitable humour, Zuma reduced this speculation to the non-issue he considered it to be: he brought both his wives and his fiancée to the Union Buildings shindig.

It is my submission that the media obsession about Msholozi's wives springs from envy.

In their most lucid moments, especially when the drinks take their toll and their intellectual guards are down, my educated friends confirm this theory.

When they raise issues about Msholozi's polygamy it is not because they are morally repulsed by the notion; it's just that they admire a man who, in this day and age, has not only the chutzpah, but also the energy to say 'I do!', not once, not twice, but four times.

I also know that many white brothers who raise issues about Msholozi's polygamous ways are not necessarily opposed to the notion of having two or three wives.

In fact, many of them have their 'roll-ons' (township argot for mistresses; you know, you put your roll-on under your armpit. Get it?).

Were many of our men to have their way, they would have more than one wife.

It's just that they are dead scared of their wives and their litigious ways.

Secondly, many are so immersed in their stressful work — what with all those long lunches soaked in whisky and wine — that to them the word libido only exists in the dictionary. Against this background, therefore, they envy Msholozi his sexual prowess. It should be recalled that during his rape trial he testified that, though he was already in his mid-sixties, he could still go for 15 minutes with a woman young enough to be his daughter. Lawd have mercy!

Sweating in envy, the brothers shook their heads ruefully and muttered: 'Lord, how does he do it? Give us a portion of your potent potion, oh great Msholozi!'

Their wives and girlfriends sighed resignedly: 'If only my poor Jim could ask Msholozi for the right muti to last just five minutes; is that asking too much of him? Just a lousy five …'

Because they can't get legally laid as often, and with as many partners as Msholozi can, the brothers have other outlets for their sexual frustrations.

Years ago I worked in an advertising agency. One of the first things I learned there as a copywriter is that sex sells. Big time.

You could be doing a print ad for a bag of rivets — but no, don't just put a bag of rivets in the picture. Liven up the ad, put a scantily clad damsel in the picture — the bustier the better.

The working man who needs the rivets will be drawn to the picture and will spend more time looking at the damsel than at the rivet. A rivet is a rivet is a rivet.

You could be selling a car — but put that in the background; in the foreground have a leggy blonde strutting her stuff. Or wrap the near-naked girl around the bonnet of the car. You will have the men murmuring 'Hhhm, what a machine!' But they will be referring to the girl, not the car. Sex sells.

Human beings generally love that which they can't have.

And men love the sex they can't have. So, the more you put it in their faces the angrier and more frustrated they get.

That's exactly the case with Msholozi. All these sex-starved men look at his burgeoning collection of women and they go berserk: the guy is having all that which they can't legally have.

In the vicissitudes of that reality, they start throwing jibes at him, the cowards.

Just in case Mrs K reads this: Baby, I am not in that gutter of envious men. I am happy with what the Lord has offered.

You see, as an African man, I will be the first to confirm that it is hard enough work to get married to one woman, let alone two or three.

Because we live in this culturally diverse country, those of us of a darker hue have to get married twice to the same woman — we do the white/western shindig, and then we top it up with the long, onerous African gig. No matter how many university degrees you have, you simply have to slaughter the required beasts and do all the African dancing and singing stuff.

Even Madiba (Mandela) did it. And Madiba did all the right things, right?

As my good friend Ndumiso Ngcobo reminds us in his recent book, "Is It Coz I'm Black"?, when a white person gets married to his beloved, he will invite some members of the immediate family and friends. They have a quiet thingamajig at a church or magistrate's court, after which they crack a couple of wine bottles and, if they feel like it, have a small braai.

A few hours down the line, the whole thing is finished. Maybe a few days later they go to Mauritius for a honeymoon. They are husband and wife.

Whoa, get the African couple!

Boy meets girl, and girl tells parents about boy. Boy's delegation is sent to the girl's home to suggest that the girl is now of marriageable age and, therefore, with these cows, we would like to take her hand in marriage.

A lot of haggling follows, over a period that can take months. Finally, the day is appointed ... oh, before the big day there are a number of mini-ceremonies where a lot of beasts are slaughtered and bottles of booze consumed, and a lot of invective exchanged between the two sides.

On the day of the wedding proper, the whole township comes to witness the spectacle. The girl is resplendent in the most expensive gown in town, and she wants even her enemies — especially her enemies — to see her in her finery.

There's a limo to take them to church; there's a huge marquee, beasts are slaughtered and there are mounds of meat to be eaten. The feasting lasts the whole weekend. More invective is exchanged between the two sides. And that's just part one.

Part two takes place the next weekend: the two parties trek to the would-be groom's parental home. This time around, things are 'traditional' — no wedding gown this time. Traditional attire — which might come in the form of West African dashikis or simply the leopard skins that are so beloved, especially of the Zulus.

Again, God's cows and goats are put to the knife. More invective is exchanged between the two parties. The bride's drunken uncle will, at the slightest provocation, remind whoever cares to listen that the bride is highly educated, and therefore the ilobolo that was paid in her honour was not commensurate with her educational achievements: 'We need another cow! You never finished paying ilobolo, you uneducated barbarians!'

And so it goes. With all the meat having been eaten, the would-be bride is not yet a bride until an old man from the groom's side smears goat's bile on her face and wrists. By the time the couple settle down in their own house, they are flat broke and angry with each other. But hey, this is tradition, brother. Things must be done the proper African way, or you will sire children with all manner of disabilities, so it is believed.

It is against this background that I think many of my educated brethren look at Msholozi and succumb to paroxysms of rage; anger that they are lesser men than he who has endured the ilobolo rites so many times — and always comes out of the process in high spirits, singing and dancing as if nothing has happened.

As for the white brothers, as I have said, they are simply envious that they can't tell their Mrs Smiths and Vermeulens that, hey, look, skattie, I want to take a second wife who can help with the, um you know what, while you darn my socks and undies.

I can imagine that in their minds they hold these fantasies — but some fantasies are better left in the world of fantasy. Because they can turn into nightmares in the hands of less gifted men, like those who are barking from the peripheries, enviously wondering aloud how Msholozi, at 67, manages.

Leave the man to his mission, and his Umshini. Which takes us, readily and logically, to the next chapter…

17 May 2009

Flirt till you hurt!

WITH BOREDOM GETTING the better of me the other day I turned to my TV for some respite — as a last resort, I might add. As soon as I started channel surfing I stumbled upon what promised to be an interesting programme on BBC Entertainment.

What stopped me dead in my tracks was the title of the programme — Coupling.

Like a schoolboy about to raid the cookie jar I felt highly excited, and lowered the volume, just in case my wife was listening to the voices that normally come with movies with such interesting titles as Coupling. I looked around the room to check what Mrs K was doing. I had to check because the coupling that I thought was going to take place on Coupling would be objectionable to Mrs K. I know her.

To my relief, I noticed that Mrs K was sitting in a corner, with her back to the TV screen, involved in earnest telephonic conversation.

But then my heart began to sink when it turned out that the coupling that I thought would take place on Coupling was not the kind of coupling that had set my heart racing in the first place. So I raised the volume again.

It was an innocent sitcom — but with that quintessentially English style of humour so dry you could grab a chunk of it, dunk it into your hot cup of coffee and enjoy it.

The story, in a nutshell: boy has exchanged telephone numbers with girl. Mustering his courage, he phones said girl one evening. On the screen we see her picking up the receiver and getting highly excited on recognising his voice. But then there is a long pause from his end. It's not your 'I'm-gathering-my-thoughts' kind of pause. It's an 'I-have-hit-verbal-cul-de-sac' kind of pause. It's an 'I-don't-know-why-I-called' kind of pause. It's a 'can-someone-come-save-me-from-this-mess' kind of pause.

We see the guy sweating on the screen – huge beads of sweat the size of grapes. The girl keeps prompting him calmly from the other end, 'I know you're there, keep talking.'

Anyway, this vignette got me thinking about what I have written previously about men who are envious of President Jacob Zuma's bevy of women. Some men who have written to me have confirmed that, if they had their way, and the money, of course, they would take more than one wife.

But what I want to aver here is that, apart from money, there is another thing that stops men from making moves: they are bloody scared of women!

If found in a precarious position — in a social setting where they can't flash their beautiful car to make a statement to the woman in question; or buy an inappropriately expensive bottle of wine — they are simply powerless; they don't have the confidence, and requisite verbal skills.

When I was a younger man, 'selling' yourself to a woman was a skill; it was called ukushela. And those who were good at it were called amasoka — people who, like Zuma, could charm their way into a woman's heart with disarming ease.

Those of us who were not good at the practice had to listen carefully when amasoka spoke; we had to pick the morsels of poetry from amasoka. White people call these morsels of poetry 'pick-up lines'.

For example, if a Xhosa guy encountered a beautiful lady, he would shout: 'Bli bli mntakamama, mthunzi wam wokuphumla, sambleni sam selanga (Oh, my mother's daughter, you are my pleasant shady place of rest, my umbrella)'.

Or, as jazz bassist Johnny Dyani would have said: 'Bli bli, mntanam uyagula, iyeza lakho ndim (My girl, you are very sick, and I am the medicine)!'

A Zulu guy would say: 'Umuhle engathi ugeza ngobisi, usule ngopholoni (Ah, your skin is so tender, it looks as if you wash with milk, and towel off with slices of polony)'.

The lady in question would smile in appreciation. When her guard was down, the foxy chap would pounce immediately, conquering her in a verbal contest.

I know, I know, translated into English, some of these morsels of poetry sound silly. But you must remember that milk, cheese and polony were prized items in poor black communities. So, to wash with milk ... wow! That's why, to this day, black boys who go to multiracial schools, or who live in the suburbs, are called Chizboys. Cheese is still a rare and expensive commodity in the black community at large. It's something looked at with awe and envy.

To get back to the story, in a township setting, when you saw a lady crossing the road you waved at her urgently, ran across the road at the risk of being hit by speeding taxis and, when you finally caught up with her, you'd say: 'Sorry, I seem to think I know you from somewhere.'

When she said: 'No, you don't,' you'd make the quick move: 'Ah, well, let's get to know each other.'

But there are tricky ones, especially when the woman in question is herself a wit.

For example:

Uncertain Boy: 'You are so beautiful I think together we can make a beautiful pair of angels in heaven.'

Feisty Female: 'But we have to die before we go to heaven.'

Or something like this: Nervous Uncertain Boy: 'I think we were made for each other. Our hearts are already thudding in unison ...'

Feisty Female: 'I think yours is, right now, beating so fast it wants to fall out of your mouth. Please don't die on me.'

Uncertain Boy: 'Lady, I can't sleep, I cannot eat. Please say yes to my entreaty and put me out of my misery.'

Feisty Female: 'I say yes — go see a doctor.'

When Julius Malema was spotted sidling up to Zuma's daughter, Duduzile Zuma, at her 27th birthday party some time ago I couldn't help imagining his pick-up line: 'Comrade Birthday Gal, in the interest of the National Democratic Revolution, maybe we should form a coalition ... of a romantic nature, that is. With our sticks of Cuba's best we shall smoke Helen Zille out of her office, we shall drown the Shikota party in our rivers of Moët & Chandon, we shall screech the tyres of our Mercs on the Unisa campus, making that place ungovernable until they get rid of Barney Pityana, the principal of that university who happens to have political allegiances to the newly-formed party, Cope, an "opportunistic" break-away from the ANC.

'Will you say "Viva" to that? I feel a revolution stirring within the depths of myself, comrade! Please restrain me with your hug, and shut my mouth with your lips, comrade! I grant you that mandate.'

But some chaps are quite brutal. A cat bumps into a woman sporting a wedding ring and starts expressing his amorous intentions; when the woman tries to fob him off, saying, 'But can't you see I am married to someone?' he retorts: 'Yes, of course you are married to some person. A woman of your beauty can't be married to a dog.'

One of my best-loved composers, the gentle soul of jazz, Duke Ellington, was marvellous at pick-up lines. One of his favourites was: 'Girl, you make that dress look so beautiful.' Another was: 'I didn't know angels could be so luscious.

So, I still say: you envy Zuma not only for his bevy of women, but also for his charm. Go learn the tricks, men! Come to think of it, why is it that men always have to make the first move? In a democratic, non-sexist, non-racist, non-patriarchal, non-every-thing South Africa, the women should start making the first moves. Men are tired of embarrassing themselves.

24 May 2009

Eat well, go to the gym, die young and leave a good-looking corpse

PERHAPS KEEPING TO THEIR NEW YEAR'S resolutions, the punters are back in droves at the gym. Needless to say, yours truly has also emerged from a festive-season-induced hiatus during which a great many battles were waged against Bacchus's bottles.

Because my body is stiff from the long break, I am spending more time at the gym looking at other people's bodies than putting mine back into its former glorious shape.

Just look at these people. There's this guy who gives black people a bad name. He is huge, tall and has an ugly tummy that goes widdle-waddle, widdle-waddle as he battles his way through a routine on the treadmill.

His arms are boulders - not in a toned, come-and-touch-me manner but in a manner reminiscent of a gorilla's arms. And they are hairy too! The kind of guy I would not bring to my children's playroom unless I wanted the little ones to have heart attacks.

He's got a big head too, bald, and a face carved carelessly like the face of Mount Kilimanjaro. Don't talk about his nostrils; they are flared as if he is trying his damndest to out-breathe other human beings on earth.

And then there are a couple of those women who give white people a bad name. They have no backsides to speak of. Their backsides are what we call "ironing boards" in township parlance. No contours whatsoever. Their chests are equally flat.

These ladies are so emaciated I sometimes think their arms will break under the weight of the tiniest of barbells. Tom Wolfe has a name for these ladies. He calls them social X-rays, not only because you can almost see through them, but also because they like to parade their spectrally thin presence at parties where they think we are looking admiringly at them, when in fact many of us are wondering how they escaped from a feeding centre in the Sudan.

And then there is this guy who is so big he is almost twice the size of Marlon Brando or Jimmy Abbott at their fattest. I look at him and wonder why he waited so long before he decided to come to the gym. To reshape that amoeboid body of his will take a miracle. I mean, the guy has boobs. Maybe those social X-ray ladies can borrow them from him.

Really, he is not a good advertisement for a gym: "Go to the gym and you'll turn out like me!"

I think the gym owners should pay him to stay at home. He is a discouragement and a distraction to those of us who believe we can still lose some fat and gain some muscle through rigorous sessions on the treadmill - when we are not looking at other people's diabolical physiques.

But hey, that's beside the point. Let's take solace in the fact that South Africans, living up to the exhortation of one medical aid scheme, now generally believe "it pays to be healthy" - yes, it pays to join this medical scheme not only because it subsidises your gym contract, but it also gives you a discount when you shop at Stuttafords and pays a portion of your movie tickets. So, if you can't go to the gym, no sweat. Go sit in a movie house and quaff Coke after Coke and gobble tons of popcorn. That's right, it pays to be healthy.

I am just wondering how many of the new and not so new visages that I have encountered at the gym are going to last. Will they still be around come Easter? Or will they have decided to use their medical aid benefits by going to the movies? Just a question.

On a more serious note, it's heartening to realise that people are worrying about their well-being: going to the gym, changing their eating habits by eliminating or reducing meat in their diets and cutting down on their concerted battles with Bacchus's bottles.

But cynics are laughing at us. The other day a meat-eating, whisky-swilling friend who doesn't go to gym and has a huge belly to prove it, pointed out that jazz pianist Alice Coltrane, who died at the weekend, was a clean-living soul who turned vegetarian in the '60s and did spiritual things like yoga and meditation which, I would think, are equivalent to going to the gym. Yet she died at the tender age of 69.

Her husband, John Coltrane, who was also vegetarian, died at 40 from liver cancer.

What these cynics forget to mention is that before going to India, where he embraced a way of living that influenced him to stop drinking and eating meat, Coltrane was a drug and alcohol addict and thus punished his liver.

The cynics also mention Jim Fixx, who turned jogging from a cult exercise in the '70s to the phenomenon of today. He died at the age of 52. And then Mark Hughes, who founded Herbalife, a company that advocates so-called natural cures, who died in his sleep at age 44.

But don't listen to the cynics. Exercising and a good diet are all about risk reduction. They do not guarantee immortality. In any case, if you are a gym goer and happen to die young, to the merriment of the cynics, you can be sure of leaving behind a good-looking corpse.

21 January 2007

Fashion Notes

Every time the Brother arrives...

LIFE IS NOT FAIR. Not at all. As a teenager perambulating the dusty streets of Mpumalanga township in Hammarsdale (township streets are always dusty, by the way), this brother used to dream of himself as a real mean gangster.

But when he got in touch with real-life gangsters he realised that he wasn't cut out for that kind of industry. He has never been in a mood to lose his teeth in a fistfight, or have his face scarred to prove a point. So he missed out on being a gangster.

And then some bright spark decided that bell-bottom trousers were fashionable. So this brother started working for white people, doing their gardens (got fired three times in three months) in an attempt to earn money so he could buy himself a pair.

By the time he had saved enough money for the bell-bottoms, the same bright spark who had introduced them had decided that they were no longer fashionable. Then they introduced Dobbshire trousers, but by the time this brother had enough money to afford them (they cost R57), they were also out of fashion.

Oh, yes, when they introduced Jack Purcell takkies, this brother was one of the first to own a pair (they cost R26). So he was finally 'with it'. By that time he had started looking around, you know, at the girls, and he thought they would notice that he was one of the first guys in the street to own a pair of Jack Purcells.

But then some arbiter of taste decided that the Jack Purcell reign should only be one year. And in any case, this brother soon discovered that it was no longer fashionable to look like a thug, a tsotsi. The so-called Pantsula phase of fashion was no longer a hit with the girls.

Somebody decided we should wear high-heeled shoes and tight-fitting pants with no pockets, and we called ourselves the Ivies. And then there was another branch of the Ivies, called the American Dudes. I suppose you would equate the Ivies to black economic empowerment types and the American Dudes to affirmative action types. Same tree, different-sized branches. Previously disadvantaged, all of them.

Anyway, I became an American Dude. But being an American Dude was quite expensive. When the tsotsis took their girlfriends to town, they would buy the poor girls a can of Coke and an apple. The American Dudes, on the other hand, were expected to buy such expensive things as steak-and-kidney pie and Yogisip. The tsotsis took their girlfriends to Scala Cinema (oooh, the bed bugs there), and we used to take our girls to Shah Jehan, or Isfahan Cinema.

For a moment one was contented, being 'up there', and enjoying the sweet life of being a fashionable guy. But the good life was not going to last: some bright spark decided that it was no longer fashionable to have a perm (oohh, the greasy permed hair that used to drive the girls crazy).

I think you are beginning to get the picture. Every time this brother thinks he has arrived, some arbiter of taste and fashion decides to pull the rug from under his shoes.

Ah, yes, when this brother discovered the likes of Chinua Achebe and the Wole Soyinkas of this world and thought reading them would make him sound revolutionary, somebody decided it was no longer fashionable or revolutionary enough to read these writers. To show your revolutionary spirit you had to go into exile.

Now, this brother loves ideas and stuff, but he's never been in love with the words 'fight' and 'die'. So he decided, 'Nah, I ain't going to exile even if it's fashionable.' But when this brother decided to become a journalist — so that he could be quoted like Can Themba and Nat Nakasa and Damon Runyon — he discovered it was no longer fashionable to be quoted. All you needed was a quotable bank balance. And a lookable car.

Well, the journey continued. When the brother started wearing spectacles so he could look educated and intelligent, fashion editors created a new word to offend the brother: they called him a nerd. Hhawu! Then, when the brother thought he had reached the pinnacle of visibility he bought a 4x4 and a convertible. Now the brother has been told about climate change, which brings with it very chilly winters; what's the point of having a convertible car when you can't drive it with the roof down? And this week the brother was told that 4x4s are going to be phased out. Just when he was beginning to enjoy them. Okay, they are not being phased out, but the powers that be have decided that 4x4 drivers should be charged what is called a green tax. Now, tax of any colour doesn't appeal to this brother. They say 4x4s are having an effect on climate change. But there is no proof. If the government were serious about imposing an environmental tax, it would be advised to enforce emission standards rather than obsess over size. Size matters in many other things, but not this time around. Can you please allow some brothers and sisters the pleasure of driving their big cars? If there is a threat to the environment, it should be the taxis. Go for the taxi drivers, for Allah's sake.

27 May 2007

If the shoe doesn't fit...

THERE IS SOMETHING ABOUT MEN AND THEIR SHOES. They are not just foot covers. They are a projection of an identity.

That's why many streetwise men sniggered and shook their heads in sympathy when Mbeki made that joke of his about Mandela and his shoes. When asked if he wasn't humbled by the prospect of filling the big shoes of Mandela, Zizi retorted that he wouldn't be stepping into the old man's shoes — the Old Man, the Short Man said, wore ugly shoes in the first place.

Little did the Short Man realise that sooner or later he would fall victim to the Shower* Man's shoes: boom, a nicely polished shoe on his behind.

Coming from a township, as I do, I know what shoes say about men, or about the mood they are in. Many streetwise women from the townships can give you a thorough lesson on what the shoes men wear say about them. A guy can be handsome, with the body of a hunk and the smile of the rising sun, but if he's got on the 'wrong' shoes, oops, he's out Joe, as we say in my neck of the woods.

In assessing a compatible mate — and don't ask me where this comes from, it's just the way it is — women look at the shoes and then the belt, and then 'Aah' they sigh in contentment, and are prepared to speak to the guy.

Another rule about shoes: when you are wearing black shoes, you can't leave your house wearing a brown belt. No good, dude. I don't know who made this rule, but shoes must match the colour of your belt. And the belt is itself a fashion statement, a projection of one's image and style. It's gotta stand out.

When my father was a younger man and in charge of a second-division soccer club back in the days, he had a variety of shoes for various occasions.

When he wore his brown suede Barker shoes to the game I knew immediately that he expected there would be a fight in the stands. So he needed a sharp-pointed shoe that could do some damage to an adversary. But the shoe also had a conveniently thin sole, so he could easily show them a clean pair of soles if the occasion demanded. Pragmatic man, my father. You kick them, or you, ahem, show them a clean pair of soles. After all, that clean pair of soles was beautifully designed to be displayed to admirers as the occasion demanded.

My father learned a lot about shoe style from my Uncle Ernest, who had a vast collection of shoes. There were what he called sh*t-kickers – thick dull shoes he wore when he went to a particularly rough street brawl but there were also some dainty Florsheim Viking shoes, which he wore when he wanted to be seen traipsing down the streets of Chesterville township near Durban.

There were other brands for the upstarts, such as Nunn Bush, and, of course, the ubiquitous Crockett & Jones. And many more. There were shoes for going to church, to the game, to the girls, to work, to a fight. That's Uncle Ernest's style for you. Uncle Ernest would have disapproved of the fellow who threw his shoes at George W Bush. Show some respect for your shoes; don't throw them at Bush.

I can't speak much about the shoe preferences of guys from the rural areas — the shoes that I've seen in Cofimvaba in the Eastern Cape and Malamulele in the Venda area speak eloquently about the types of men who come from rural areas. Which isn't much. 'Nuff said.

I also cannot speak eloquently about the Ventersdorp types with their grey shoes that look as if they were purchased from Morkels, 'your two-year guarantee store'. Or the veldskoene of the Karoo. Or the nondescript Hush Puppies that the English-speaking okes from suburbs and estates such as Kloof, Nottingham Road and Malvern wear — bought on their behalf from Shoprite Checkers by the wife while she was busy capitalising on the latest spaghetti sale, thanks to the mercifulness of those shifty okes Finance Minister Trevor Manuel and Reserve Bank Governor Tito Mboweni (hey, that sounds like a crooked law firm: M&M Associates).

My chinas from Chatsworth and Laudium and Lenasia, they prefer open sandals, I tune you. Wearing shoes for them is too much of a hassle. Every now and then they have to take off their shoes, in any case, so they can pray to their god, you see. So, heavy shoes are a hassle, you see mamoo?

My cousins from Macassar, Mitchells Plain, Westbury and Wenties … I don't know what it is they wrap around their feet. Sometimes they dress as if they are straight out of the Bronx or some gaudy American ghetto, with all those yellow and red and orange and green takkies, and their T-shirts emblazoned with messages such as Born To Die, or Ama-Kip-Kip. I mean, that's fashion sacrilege. Yuck! Where do these guys get these fashion monstrosities from?

And there is this new South African man: the BEE type. This one doesn't know whether he's coming or going — is he township, or is he northern suburbs? And the shoes he wears are a manifestation of this indecision. Wait a minute, now, it's beginning to dawn on me: the shoes that the BEE type wears are so sharply pointed that they, are, in fact, saying to you: 'I can only go forward ... and UP'. Their noses are so sharply pointed they can smell a tender from afar.

Take a mampara from Transkei or Mqanduli or Mgezankamba and dress him in these sharp pointed shoes. In no time at all, he will tell you where the next tender is. He will go for it, kicking everybody out of the way, if that's what he has to do in order to get to it. And once he's got it, he can only tolerate others wearing the same kind of shoe to sit around the trough.

So, the BEE brother taps his sharp shoes as he tucks into salmon and sauvignon blanc. Except that he pronounces it sal-mon, and sa-vig-non blank.

And you with your grey shoes from Ventersdorp or veldskoene from the Karoo, Florsheims from Lamontville or Ama-Kip-Kip from Westbury, are out, broer.

Out, and you shall stay there. And eat your lousy Christmas and New Year there.

28 December 2008

Town Talk syndrome all over again

DURING THE '70S of my childhood the festive season was remarkable: older people, groaning under the weight of money which they called Bonus, were overly generous, tossing a coin in one's direction at the slightest provocation.

You didn't have to spin yet another yarn about your school teacher needing money to buy chlorophyll for a class science experiment.

Their generosity also saw them buying new clothes for their piccaninnies and themselves — the shiniest Dobbshire pants here, Florsheim shoes with the thickest soles you could get there, fancy Viyella shirts — the works.

But the highlight was when your parents took possession of a new Welcome Dover coal stove and a lounge suite, complete with gumba-gumba music player, from Town Talk Furnishers.

You would try to make the most of this new lounge suite because, come January or February, the people from Town Talk would come — to collect it.

Your parents would be so impatient and angry you couldn't risk asking why the people from Town Talk were repossessing the furniture.

It was much later in life that I cottoned on that people knowingly ordered these huge lounge suites that they could not afford just to impress their neighbours and visitors over the festive season, to show that they had moved up the ladder of respectability.

Those days, furniture stores were not as sophisticated as they are today; they couldn't take you to the credit bureau for non-payment, so the best they could do was repossess the motley collection of furniture that they had supplied to you on a hire-purchase basis. By the time they came, some of the chairs would be so threadbare they might have been with you for the whole decade.

Needless to say, I detested the white people from Town Talk for their hard-heartedness; why mess with the parents' image in the 'hood?

My parents were among the first in our neighbourhood to have their furniture repossessed. But it soon became a fashion; the other darkies caught up with the wily ways of the Khumalos.

The repossession of furniture by the hard-hearted white Town Talkers was brought back to my mind by a newspaper report this week which said the black middle class, the so-called Black Diamonds, who make up 9% of the population, now account for 28% of all spending.

The Black Diamonds, a survey quoted by the paper showed, are expected to exceed spending by whites by 2009. Nothing wrong with that. The problem is that the Black Diamonds are overspending, especially on luxury items such as cars. And the cars are getting repossessed.

Now therein lies the rub. It's '70s black South Africa all over again — with the Town Talk furniture people appearing in a new incarnation: they are now BMW, Jeep, etcetera.

The Black Diamonds, who earn, on average, R6 100 a month, have no compunction about buying an expensive vehicle, knowing very well that a few months down the line it will be repossessed because of non-payment. The thinking seems to be: As long as people have seen me driving it, it's fine, those heartless people at BMW or the bank can come take it away.

I know of a famous filmmaker who has the whole thing down to a fine art. Because he has a clean credit record, and often gets huge amounts from the SABC to make TV productions, he goes to a car dealership, chooses one of the latest models, charms the sales team, gets a bank to finance the deal and ends up driving away in a beautiful car.

That'll be the last the bank hears from him; no repayments whatsoever. Just when the bank is about to report him to the credit bureau — the brother has good timing! — he drives the car back to the dealership, pleading poverty: 'I've lost my contract with the SABC, blah, blah.'

I believe this scam, if I should call it that, has caught on countrywide.

Not long ago I wrote a column encouraging my brethren, especially the educated ones, to take pride in the cars they drive.

For my sins, I was chewed out by some of my readers, who said I was encouraging irresponsible spending. All I was trying to say is that driving a beautiful car in an impoverished neighbourhood you grew up in would show the young guns there that beautiful wheels are not the preserve of gangsters.

That is all I said. I never said that people should spend money they don't have in order to impress. I never said people should get into trouble with their banks and the credit bureaus.

And God forfend, don't try to be South Africa's self-styled answer to Paris Hilton, socialite Khanyi Mbau; you don't know where her money comes from (if it's still there).

And, for crying out loud, I never said people should steal in order to finance wheels or any other possessions that might impress their friends and their dog. Cars, by the way, are not an investment; you buy an expensive car once you have investments.

Don't do what our parents used to do, that is, buy furniture on hire purchase in an attempt to spite the white people at Town Talk Furnishers.

17 June 2007

Of This And That

Aggression is the better part of valour in the US

I'VE ALWAYS BEEN FASCINATED BY American valour — everything from the gun-slingers of the Wild West to present-day East Coast vs West Coast street wars featuring gangs such as the Crips and the Bloods.

Every now and then this American determination to spill blood, even for the wrong reasons, will grab the public imagination with such force that an observer can't help but ask himself: really, where do these Americans come from?

Something happened this past weekend that got me asking myself the same question. As a result, I found myself rereading a chapter which centres on the birth of New Orleans, the city that epitomises Americanism because of its multicultural and blood-spattered history.

Herbert Asbury, that great documenter of US American popular history, in his Gangs of New Orleans, relates a couple of early incidents in New Orleans history which make some interesting points about the Americans' willingness to spill blood at the slightest provocation.

One night six young Creoles, he writes, were walking along the deserted streets of New Orleans when one exclaimed: 'Oh, what a beautiful night! What splendid level ground for a joust! Suppose we pair off, draw our swords, and make this night memorable by a spontaneous display of bravery and skill!'

The good idiots thereupon fought until two of their number lay dead upon the field.

But this only deepened the city's obsession with the culture of duels.

In 1817 Bernard Marigny, one of the city's famous duellists, was elected to the state legislature. One day he delivered an impassioned speech to which one James Humble responded dismissively.

Offended, Marigny challenged Humble to a duel.

Humble's friends said if he refused to pick up the gauntlet he would surely lose his social standing. Under pressure, but still reluctant to fight, Humble wrote a missive to his adversary: 'I accept your challenge, and in the exercise of my privilege I stipulate that the duel shall take place in Lake Pontchartrain in six feet of water, sledgehammers to be used as weapons.'

The problem was that Marigny was less than five feet eight inches tall. He was also so slight he could scarcely lift a sledgehammer. But his friends urged him to stand on a box and run the risk of having his skull cracked by Humble's hammer.

Exasperated, Marigny declared that it was impossible for him to fight a man with such a sense of humour. He apologised to Humble, and the two became firm friends.

Americans are a complex lot. A crazy lot. A funny lot. They get more dangerous when they are desperate. Remember what they did to the poor people of Afghanistan when they couldn't locate Osama bin Laden?

Needless to say, they still haven't found their man. But they haven't given up. They will do everything to make up for this shortcoming.

Dick Cheney, the US Vice-President and a true patriot, acted in the spirit of a desperate American last weekend.

It seems to me that Bin Laden has been occupying Cheney's thoughts of late and he desperately wanted to do something about it. When the 'aha!' moment hit him, he gathered a couple of friends and decided to go hunting for quail at a ranch in Texas.

Some time during the hunting session the hunters repaired to a lounge, where they downed a couple of beers. Cheney decided it was time to perform his patriotic duty and 'do something' about Bin Laden.

When the hunting resumed, he peppered one Harry M Whittington with birdshot.

The White House, after some deep thinking, told the public that Cheney had mistaken Whittington for a bird.

But more reliable sources tell us that there was some logic behind the shooting. Immediately after discharging his gun at Whittington, Cheney had sent this message to the White House: 'We can't get Bin Laden, but we nailed a 78-year-old attorney. At least one is doing something about this Bin Laden fella.'

Or at least that's how CBS television presenter David Letterman recounts the story.

The lawyer was making a good recovery in hospital when Cheney and friends decided to pay him a visit. Upon laying his eyes on Cheney, Whittington was seized by a heart attack.

The fact that the White House took time before going public about the shooting incident and the fact that everything in the US is subject to a conspiracy theory, leads many observers there to see the shooting as not having been an accident at all.

Jeff Nussbaum, a Washington speechwriter, has an interesting take on this.

'The idea that you have this vice-president who is kind of gruff and willing to cuss out senators meant that it was always within the realm of possibility that he would go off one day and shoot his friend,' he says. 'This really is a perfect metaphor for an administration that shoots first and then blames the victim later.'

Nussbaum goes on to point out that the cause of the so-called accident is far deeper and says something about America under Bush: 'It was faulty intelligence: the CIA assured [Cheney] that Harry Whittington was actually a pheasant.'

Yes, American valour fascinates me — especially when it misses its target.

19 February 2006

The ilobolo mystery

THE GROOM'S PARTY WERE IN HIGH SPIRITS as they left for the bride's home, where they would be delivering thousands of rands in lobolo.

To represent the groom in these generally intricate, make-or-break negotiations about the future of the young couple is always an honour.

Only the best raconteurs and strategists are chosen as abakhongi, or negotiators. You have to be tough without being rude during the talks.

On the first day, for example, the girl's father might chase the abakhongi with a stick, shouting: 'Ngikhulisa ingane, nina senibona umfazi. Demelayisi (I'm still raising my child, and you are already seeing a woman in her. Damned rice! — a potent Zulu epithet).'

On some occasions, the father might simply sulk and not say a word until someone has the presence of mind to produce the money — sometimes as little as R100 — called imvulamlomo (literally, 'the mouth-opener'). The talking will start. The process can take weeks, or even months, to-ing and fro-ing.

Concluding the process is therefore an immense achievement. Yes, traipsing down the aisle, to the adulation of family members, friends and relatives, and of course the undying envy of former lovers and rivals, is the highlight of any woman's life — or man's, for that matter. You have every reason to celebrate with the finest ring you can afford.

But lobolo is even more sacred than the ring itself because it brings the two families together, invoking ancestors from both sides to bless the newlyweds and look after them on behalf of God.

Most Africans, even those who have embraced Western ways and Christianity, still swear by their lobolo, which, of course, has been refined in many ways. Some take it crudely as 'bride price' — buying a bride — while those who are honest to their culture see it as a process of cementing the bonds between the families.

In the latter case, the money paid by the groom goes towards paying for the lavish wedding party that comes after the walk down the church aisle; in the former case, unfortunately, the money disappears into the bottomless pockets of the bride's parents, who will expect the poor lad also to finance the lavish party and start a home for the newlyweds. Intimations of future problems!

But let's not go there.

Let's go back to our groom's party as they walked towards the bride's home where they would pay lobolo.

The men in question were from a township on the East Rand. On their way they were intercepted by a group of thugs.

Interestingly, the thugs did not waste time searching all six of them.

They went straight to the guy who carried the booty, making off with the money. Curious, the other members of the party thought, as they later sat down to review the day's events. How had the criminals known who was carrying the money?

It transpired that the groom, who had stayed at home while his emissaries went about their mission, as per tradition, had masterminded the mugging. He had told the thugs that the man with the money would be wearing a white coat.

Seems to me he planned to go to his in-laws with the sorry tale and ask for an extension while he saved more money. Buying time.

This story was told to me by a colleague as we exchanged notes about lobolo and things people have done with this sacred ritual. The spark for the discussion was a story in the Sowetan newspaper.

Kenneth Mdakana, the story said, dispatched his emissaries to the home of his sweetheart, Keketso Kabasia, making sure to load them with R10 000 as lobolo. Impressive.

As the parties sat down to count the money one of Mdakana's uncles realised that the would-be groom had given them fake notes! Fake money for lobolo — the height of insolence! The guy should have pleaded poverty or even offered to pay in Zim dollars. You can buy three tomatoes for Z$60-billion, but at least Zim dollars would represent sincerity of intent.

I sympathise with the brothers: Tito is giving us all a hard time — witness the 4x4s on auction and the For Sale signs in the suburbs.

But there are limits, brothers. Robbing lobolo of its dignity is like a Jew urinating inside the synagogue, or a Seventh Day Adventist drinking alcohol on the Sabbath, or a Muslim eating pork inside the mosque. Peace, baf'ethu!

3 August 2008

A Zulu delicacy with some unpronounceable names

'**YOU CAN PERHAPS CONSIDER CHANGING THE NAME**,' my colleague suggested coolly, 'then I might consider trying the meat.'

We were standing around my workstation waxing lyrical about the delicious meat of thryonomys swinderianus, which, for a long time has been enjoyed by a small exclusive group of members of South African society. Now there are attempts to move this delicacy into the mainstream.

Over the past few years delights such as crocodile, snake, etc – which have been enjoyed by real connoisseurs – have moved onto the menus of top restaurants all over the country.

Through food, as through fashion, you can make a political statement. I am so and so, therefore, I eat this. But also, accessibility to food is driven by socio-economic realities.

As far back as 10 years ago a unit at the University of Natal had started experimenting with introducing thryonomys swinderianus meat as the cheapest form of protein – a socio-economic reality was being grappled with there. I remember reporting gleefully on this bold initiative.

In West Africa the meat is a long established delicacy, and I believe some South American countries swear by it.

The talk I was having with colleagues about meat and other affordable forms of protein was sparked by two things: first a story pointing out that snakes had been wreaking havoc on a farm in Hluhluwe, eating the little thryonomys swinderianus being bred there as part of an experimental scheme which will culminate in the little lovely creatures being introduced into restaurants all over the country.

The second thing that sparked the talk was an article in our sister newspaper, Business Day, which, in its analysis of the fortunes of one chicken-processing company, noted: 'Chicken remains one of the cheapest forms of protein. It therefore holds that when disposable income levels increase and people can afford more meat in their diets, poultry is among the first in line.'

I agreed with the sentiment, but went on further to point out that thryonomys needs to be exploited as the cheapest form of protein.

Having written at some length about thryonomys, perhaps it is time I introduced my friend in more languages than one. The little creature under question is very cuddly when alive, and very tasty when dead and, in my native isiZulu, we call it ivondwe.

The uncouth members of society, those who insist on calling escargot 'snails', will tell you that my little friend is called a cane rat.

But this is not a rat! It can be found in lush grasslands and, of course, sugar cane plantations.

I think the meat of ivondwe is closer to that of a rabbit than anything I've ever tasted. Even in its design the ivondwe is closer to the rabbit than to the rat. It is certainly smaller than the rabbit, but, like the rabbit, it has no tail.

It's been a while since I last tasted ivondwe meat. When I was growing up in KwaZulu-Natal my father would catch them and boil them for us. Sometimes he would braai them – ivondwe elosiwe.

My younger siblings, of course, missed out, because by the time their eyes opened we had already moved to the township where amavondwe were nowhere to be found. In the township the new delicacy was izimbiba, little brown rats with striped backs. Okay, these were closer relatives to the rats. But let's not allow izimbiba to distract us.

We are talking about amavondwe, thryonomys. Above I pointed out that what you eat can be taken as a political statement; or what you eat can be determined by socio-economic realities.

In France, for example, 'brown rats and roof rats were eaten openly on a large scale in Paris when the city was under siege during the Franco-Prussian War. Observers likened their taste to both partridges and pork. And, according to the Larousse Gastronomique, rats are still eaten in some parts of France, writes Calvin W Schwabe in his book Unmentionable Cuisine (Charlottesville, Virginia: University of Virginia Press 1979).

The book goes on to give a variety of recipes. 'Grilled Rats Bordeaux Style' (Entrecôte à la bordelaise). 'Alcoholic rats inhabiting wine cellars are skinned and eviscerated, brushed with a thick sauce of olive oil and crushed shallots, and grilled over a fire of broken wine barrels.' And so on and so on …

The French are known to eat frog legs as well, but I don't know which war necessitated this experiment, which has stayed on the French menu to this day.

We are fortunate to be a multicultural society, which means that not only do we speak in many tongues, but our tongues sing praises to a variety of dishes.

There are people among us who prize caviar. I have tried it on a number of occasions. Had I been told right from the onset that caviar was nothing but fish eggs,

I think I wouldn't have bothered.

Then there are Italian people among us who eat sheep's brain mixed with tripe. I've tried this and found it delicious.

Where I grew up – Mpumalanga township, near Hammarsdale – in the kingdom of the Zulus, we had a sizeable community of BaSotho people. We found it odd that they ate cats and horsemeat, while they found it odd that we ate izimbiba and rabbits.

But now that we are a rainbow nation, it's time to take this spirit of multiculturalism to culinary fronts. Ivondwe is the farm animal of the future.

28 November 2004

Braced for the fair, boots and all

NO MATTER HOW WORLD-WEARY or emotionally detached you may be from reality, a time will come in your life that will make you feel, once again, like a child: excitable, easy to please, open-minded. Even if only for a fleeting moment.

The child in me was roused from the long slumber of cynicism the other day when my good friend and colleague BBK brought me a gift - a spanking new pair of soccer boots. These were not just ordinary soccer boots in commonplace black leather with white trim and white studs. These boots were from outer space, or from beyond the Pearly Gates. These are the boots Gabriel and his comrades yonder wear when they take to the field.

They remind me of a work Picasso would have produced during his cubism period - bizarre cut fragments of leather painted in stroboscopic colours: red, lime, navy, black, yellow. If I were to be given occasion to wear my new boots at night, I would solve Eskom's problems: the streets would be ablaze.

Anyway, no sooner had BBK presented me with the boots - right at the office - than I took off my own shoes and put on my new acquisitions. Ah, I was walking on air. I suddenly had the urge to go and drink coffee. When I realised that nobody at the coffee area remarked on the heavenly babes on my feet, I decided to leave the jealous losers alone. I went and joined colleagues who were having a smoke on the balcony - I don't smoke, mind you, but I don't mind being a passive smoker if there's a message I want to deliver ...

Sadly, my friends who wield cancer sticks were too engrossed in prattle about newspaper circulation to even notice my boots. Recalling one of my younger brother's tricks when he wanted to draw attention to a new pair of shoes or socks, I put one of my feet on a chair and started whistling joyfully as I untied and re-tied my shoelace. At last, from the corner of my eye, I noticed a colleague prodding his neighbour and nodding his head in my direction.

First there were titters, then giggles, and these finally crescendoed into outright guffaws.

When the makhulu baas spotted the boots, I thought he would recommend me for a salary increase seeing that I was setting high standards of sartorial elegance at the office. Bah! Like the rest of the unfashionable flibbertigibbets I work with, he simply said the colour of my boots confirmed what he had long suspected about me: that I was from the northern parts of this country. Or even beyond the Limpopo. Ah, what can one say about people who think Christian Dior is a new MP from the African Christian Democratic Party?

And, oh, why did BBK buy me the boots in the first place? I was one of the lucky scribes who had been invited to represent this beautiful country at the London Book Fair early this week. Because South Africa is hosting the World Cup, the organisers of the fair had been thoughtful enough to set up a friendly match between local authors and their British counterparts as one of the side attractions to the book fair.

As if being laughed at for my new boots were not enough, fate was to play a cruel joke on my ambitions to play soccer in London. On the day I was supposed to fly - April 16 - we were told that all flights into and out of London had been cancelled because of a volcano that had exploded somewhere in Iceland. Like a child who doesn't want to wake up from a dream in which Santa Claus is feeding him loads of candy, I refused to believe that some lousy ash could bring Europe to a sudden halt, and thus spoil my fun.

The poet Masoja phoned me late on Friday, sounding very dejected at having been turned away from the airport. He would have been on an earlier flight than mine.

By the following day, Saturday, because I was looking for would-be fellow denialists, I started phoning friends who were on the list of those supposed to travel to the UK. They were all depressed, but gradually beginning to make peace with the fact that the cursed ash was not a figment of someone's imagination. There was a suggestion that we should go en masse to the airport and demand to be flown somewhere in Europe where the ash hadn't presented its accursed self!

Why, one of the organisers in London itself sent us an e-mail to say it had been decided to charter a plane which would fly from Cape Town. My colleague, Phakama Mbonambi, and I were excited at this possibility - but the children in us did not allow themselves to ask the simple question: where would this lovely charter plane land, seeing that the entire miserable island of Britain had closed its miserable airspace?

Siphiwo Mahala of the Department of Arts and Culture defied all of us when he decided that he would fly from Johannesburg to Frankfurt, via Dubai. And from Frankfurt? I wanted to know. He said: "Ag, I'll see." On Sunday he sent me an SMS to say he was still stuck in Dubai.

Later that day, it was decided to have a small commiserations party for the grounded lot. By arrangement, a number of us gathered at novelist Niq Mhlongo's place. Succour came in the form of a number of bottles containing carefully distilled water from the Scottish highlands.

Experience has taught me that the famed beverages from those parts tend to flow most agreeably if accompanied by meat and meandering talk. Incidentally, a lot of this talk - passionate, profound and insightful - was about the book fair that we never attended.

Experience has also taught me that a great many things can be said about something that one knows absolutely nothing about.

Someone averred that the fair was going to be a damp squib (because these gallant, grounded scribes drinking Scottish water couldn't make it, don't you see!).

Come to think of it, it was possibly good that we were not there, continued the sage whose intellect had been fortified by the waters from the Scottish highlands.

He said the gods had intervened to save us from you-will-never-know-what.

And when the comrade writer spat out the words "the bloody book fair", and invoked the wisdom of the gods, somebody suggested that we could drink to that.

And we did.

25 April 2010